THE DIGITAL COACH

What about the coaches ? ? ?

Thanks to digital media, coaching doesn't have to be constrained by geographical and temporal boundaries. Using digital media to facilitate coaching processes, however, creates a distinct form of coaching practice that requires additional skill from the coach.

The Digital Coach contains insights based on a comprehensive, exploratory research that analysed the discussions of a 1,000-member strong online community of coaches and several interviews with coaches to understand their practical experiences of working with technology. At the same time, the book offers information, insights, and examples that can be readily used by the coaching practitioner. Based on the developments in the field, the book provides suggestions about improving the usability of coaching software, and it offers reflections on how emerging technologies like immersive Virtual Reality, Augmented Reality, and Artificial Intelligence might extend coaching practice. Whilst acknowledging the limitations and potential risks that may arise by integrating digital media in coaching, the book suggests that coaching success doesn't only depend on media capabilities, but also on the coach. The digital coach develops enhanced coaching skills and adapts coaching practice to the media in use.

The book is dedicated to the coaching practitioner who uses digital media or who is considering doing so, and is relevant for coaching supervisors, buyers of coaching services, human resource professionals, and software designers.

Stella Kanatouri has been a researcher and lecturer at Helmut Schmidt University in Hamburg, in the faculty of vocational training and organizational learning, and a professional classical ballet dancer at John Neumeier's Hamburg Ballet. Stella currently works as a research consultant and is responsible for delivering qualitative research projects for Fortune 500 companies around the world.

ROUTLEDGE-EMCC MASTERS IN COACHING AND MENTORING

Series Editors: David Clutterbuck and Irena Sobolewska
Associate Series Editors: Julie Haddock Millar and Agnieszka Bajer

This series is published in collaboration with the European Mentoring and Coaching Council (EMCC).

Routledge-EMCC Masters in Coaching and Mentoring provides critical perspectives in coaching and mentoring. It aims to avoid the overcrowded basic coaching/mentoring textbook market and focus instead on providing a toolkit for topics outside of core theory but are necessary to become a mature practitioner.

The series will appeal to those studying to obtain certificates, diplomas and masters in coaching and mentoring, alongside experienced practitioners who wish to round out their practice using selected essential reading as part of their continuous professional development.

Coaching and Mentoring in the Asia Pacific
Edited by Anna Blackman, Derrick Kon and David Clutterbuck

Coaching Supervision
Advancing Practice and Changing Landscapes
Edited by Jo Birch and Peter Welch

The Art of Listening in Coaching and Mentoring
Authored by Stephen Burt

Coaching and Mentoring for Work-Life Balance
Authored by Julie Haddock-Millar and Eliot Tom

The Digital Coach
Authored by Stella Kanatouri

THE DIGITAL COACH

Stella Kanatouri

Routledge
Taylor & Francis Group

LONDON AND NEW YORK

First published 2020
by Routledge
2 Park Square, Milton Park, Abingdon, Oxon OX14 4RN

and by Routledge
52 Vanderbilt Avenue, New York, NY 10017

Routledge is an imprint of the Taylor & Francis Group, an informa business

© 2020 Stella Kanatouri

British Library Cataloguing-in-Publication Data
A catalogue record for this book is available from the British Library

Library of Congress Cataloging-in-Publication Data
A catalog record has been requested for this book

ISBN: 978-0-367-07772-3 (hbk)
ISBN: 978-0-367-47205-4 (pbk)
ISBN: 978-0-429-02275-3 (ebk)

Typeset in Bembo
by Swales & Willis, Exeter, Devon, UK

Visit the eResources: www.routledge.com/9780367077723

To Aliki, David, Zoe & Marco

2020

This book is the publication of the doctoral dissertation that was presented to and approved by the Faculty of Humanities and Social Sciences of the Helmut-Schmidt University, University of the Federal Armed Forces, Hamburg, Germany with the title 'Mapping the technology-assisted coaching field through the lens of an online community: An exploratory study'.

The title Doctor of Philosophy in Coaching was conferred to Stella Kanatouri on 31 July 2018.

Dissertation committee:
Dean: Prof. Dr. Karin Büchter
Supervisors: Prof. Dr. Harald Geißler and
Prof. Dr. Siegfried Greif.

CONTENTS

FIGURES

TABLES

BOXES

ABBREVIATIONS

ABC	Accelerated Behaviour Change
AI	Artificial Intelligence
a.o.	Among others
AR	Augmented Reality
CAI	Cyber Anthropoethic Intelligence
CIPD	Chartered Institute of Personnel and Development
CMC	Computer-Mediated Communication
DoF	Degrees of Freedom
FOV	Field of View
GPS	Global Positioning System
GPU	Graphical Processing Units
GROW	Goal, Reality, Obstacles/Options, Way Forward
HAM-D	Hamilton Rating Scale for Depression
HCI	Human Computer Interaction
HD	High Definition
HMD	Head Mounted Display
HR	Human Resources
ICF	International Coaching Federation
iVR	immersive Virtual Reality
ML	Machine Learning
NLP	Natural Language Processing
NLP	Neuro-Linguistic Programming
PSVR	PlayStation Virtual Reality
PTSD	Post-Traumatic Stress Disorder
SMART	Specific, Measurable, Achievable, Realistic, Time-Bound
UGC	User-Generated Content
VC	Virtual Coaching

VE	Virtual Environment
VoIP	Voice over Internet Protocol
VR	Virtual Reality

FOREWORD

There is an evolving threat to the established world of coaching. That threat we call digital myopia – an unwillingness to engage with rapid developments in technology that have the capacity both to radically enhance coaching and mentoring practice and at the same time to render much basic coaching redundant. Already, Artificial Intelligence (AI) constructs are partially replacing trauma therapists. For specific applications, the AI is more accurate in diagnosis and appears to patients to be less judgemental than the human counterpart. If you think you are digitally aware and prepared for the digital future, because you work with Slack and Trello, then you are likely to receive quite a shock in the next few years. (If you don't know what Slack and Trello are, prepare for an earthquake!)

The major trends in digitally assisted coaching are Virtual Reality (VR), coachbots and Artificial Intelligence. VR has become a well validated tool for coaches, therapists, and supervisors. In early versions, such as ProReal, it creates an on-screen virtual world, which the client populates with avatars and other symbols that enable them to distance themselves from a complex situation and see it from a stranger's eyes – much in the way that constellations and psychodrama create insights. As VR evolves, it will become increasingly possible to step into this virtual world, experiencing it in even greater depth. This new, more powerful Virtual Reality will make it possible for a coach to accompany us on a journey of self-discovery – returning coaching to its mentoring roots.

Coachbots provide simple algorithms for relatively simple and frequently met business and personal issues, giving instant access to know-how and expertise in simple, linear contexts. Current applications include gathering questionnaire data from all the members of a team and carrying out basic diagnostics of team function. We shall shortly see a coachbot to help coaches plan and manage their self-development. Coachbots are of limited value in personalized, complex adaptive situations.

AI adds a whole new dimension – the capacity to adapt and learn. The more interactions it has with humans, the more patterns it observes and is able to use in decision-making. The problem is that it is unable to exercise judgement about what it learns – it cannot be *intentional* and it cannot act according to values unless these are programmed in. AI does not just reflect the biases of its programmers; it amplifies them. Hence the controversy about racial bias in AI systems that decide whether a prisoner should be given bail.

In the AI assisted future of coaching, both the client and the coach will have their digital assistant with them. The client's feelings will be transparent, because the AI will observe and diagnose facial expression and body language – enabling a much greater level of self-awareness and self-honesty than at present. The coach's AI will be able to compare the conversation in the room with previous coaching conversations with this client. The client's AI may identify that this conversation is repeating a pattern that occurs outside the room and, with the client's permission, alert the coach to this. The coach's AI will also respond to verbal clues to have relevant information available for display, when the coach says 'Have you ever heard of the drama triangle?'

In preparing for supervision, the AI will help the coach review each coaching session, highlighting moments of tension and other points that may trigger useful reflections. And of course, the supervisor will also have an AI …

There are many unknowns about this new digital world of coaching and many challenges. How do we ensure we are not overwhelmed with information we can't process? When AIs are talking to each other, how do we manage confidentiality? All of which makes this book a very timely edition to the coaching literature. The chapters bring the world of digitally enhanced coaching to life and allow the apprehensive coach to see the opportunities that lie in embracing these technologies. The critical question is not 'How will I survive in this scary new environment?' but 'How can I use these technologies to become an even better and more effective coach than I am now?'

David Clutterbuck

ACKNOWLEDGEMENTS

After carrying out my doctoral research at the Helmut-Schmidt University in Hamburg, I decided to write this book based on the insights I obtained from my study. I felt that these insights could be used to stimulate further empirical research in the field of coaching, but they could also be readily used to support the coaching practitioner and the coaching supervisor. During my research, I created and moderated an online community of coaches working with technology, and I carried out telephone interviews with experienced coaches in the field. I am so thankful to all of them for our fruitful discussions, for their time and for sharing with me so generously their experiences and insights.

I've been very lucky to have had the support of two of the most knowledgeable people in the field: I would like to express my heartfelt gratitude to Prof. Dr. Harald Geißler and Prof. Dr. Greif for supervising my research. Prof. Dr. Harald Geißler has been continuously inspiring me and encouraging me to learn more throughout these years. I am grateful for his wonderful support, patience, and mentoring and for the role he has played in my professional and personal development. I am also indebted to Prof. Dr. Siegfried Greif for his insightful and thoughtful comments and for guiding me to improve and produce a good work. I am very thankful for his patience and for our extended telephone discussions, which allowed me to clarify salient aspects of my research.

A big thank you to all the coaching software owners who have allowed me to feature their work and for giving me examples through which, I could illustrate the role that different tools play in the coaching process.

I'd like to express my gratitude to the editorial staff at Routledge. A special thanks to Matthew Ranscombe, Kristina Abbotts, and Rosie Stewart for their great support.

Writing this book has been made possible by family and friends who have given me positive energy and reassurance, and importantly, who have tolerated me during this whole time.

To David, my partner in life, I couldn't have done this if it wasn't for his endless patience and love. David, thank you so much for your enormous support throughout the entire process of writing this book, for reading my work, and for giving me feedback. Thank you for encouraging me, for being so thoughtful of me, for taking such good care of our twins, Zoë and Marco, and for being next to me every step of the way.

Finally, a big thank you to my wonderful, loving mother, Aliki. I can't thank you enough for your unconditional love, for believing in me, and for raising me to persevere in everything I do. I owe you every success I have in my life.

INTRODUCTION

For the majority of us, the time before computers and the internet is hard to imagine anymore. 'New' or otherwise called 'digital' media are ubiquitous. They have an enormous impact on all areas of human life, as they continuously transform how we interact, how we learn, how we work, how we share information and ideas. They allow us to connect with others remotely, to circulate information instantly, and to access a vast amount of information and new forms of learning. And the story goes on, technologies evolve and emerging technologies, such as Virtual and Augmented Reality and Artificial Intelligence are expanding the opportunities for learning, working, and communicating. The influence of digital media hasn't escaped coaching. Their use adds practical value to coaching delivery, as it enables wider reach to clients, and as it offers clients expanded options for selecting a coach, allowing flexibility and efficiency. Given the growing demand for coaching over the years, the practicality of digital coaching is significant, as it means that coaching can be offered to more clients, in less time and with lower cost.

Various media have been used to facilitate coaching for over 25 years, starting with telephone coaching and later extending to newer media, such as text-based and video communication. The continuously maturing technology provides manifold opportunities to digitalize coaching processes. Today, there is a broad landscape of digital tools to facilitate the coaching dialogue and to support coaching clients' reflection and problem-solving processes during or in between coaching sessions, or even in the form of self-coaching. Such tools are used, not only by coaches and clients, as well as coaches and supervisors to communicate with one another over distance, or for clients to reflect in their own time. They are also used by coaches to manage client data, as well as to provide input – such as predefined questions and other resources that coaches can use during the coaching session. Digital tools are available to support one-on-one coaching, team coaching, coaching supervision, and self-coaching.

The meaning of digital coaching encompasses all those different technological options. Digital coaching is of course, not only about technology, it means more than just adding an 'e' to coaching. The digital coach adapts practice to accommodate digital media, without compromising the quality of coaching.

So, which technological options might the digital coach have? In traditional presence coaching, practitioners use various tools and techniques to support clients' reflection, problem-solving, and goal-attainment, from the miracle question, to goal setting techniques and open-ended questions, to the empty chair technique or creative and visualization techniques. How might these techniques translate to the virtual environment? Is there a digital solution for each of them and how can it be implemented to support the coaching process? What might be gained and what might be lost when coaching tools and techniques are digitalized? What should the coach pay attention to? Can new media expand the potential of digital coaching practice, beyond the tools and techniques that are available to support traditional, face-to-face coaching?

The mediation of technology between coach and client has several implications for the coaching interaction and process. If coach and client have no visual contact with one another, as in telephone communication, or they neither see nor hear each other, as is the case with text-based communication, they rely on reduced sensory information to communicate. There is also a difference between communicating real-time, where message exchanges are spontaneous, and communicating asynchronously, where coach and client reply in their own time. In each of these modes of communication, the mediated dialogue becomes a different experience, with different qualities, bringing advantages, but also potential limitations. Yet, the absence of sensory cues doesn't necessarily make the digital coaching experience inferior to face-to-face coaching. What it does mean, is that digital coaching practice requires the coach to adapt, even though the same core coaching skills are required for the face-to-face and the digital coach. Technology requires that the coach compensates for the loss of sensory cues and adapts coaching skills to technology-mediated communication. Ethical issues that are specific to the digital form of coaching shouldn't be neglected either. Technology creates different conditions to those in face-to-face coaching. Ensuring confidentiality when working with an AI, data breaches when communicating via the web and establishing boundaries for digital coaching interactions are examples of issues that may arise when computer-mediated communication is involved, and they may look different than the ethical issues that need to be addressed to protect clients in traditional coaching processes. All these make digital coaching a rather distinct form of coaching from traditional, face-to-face coaching.

Perhaps for these reasons, coaches who are used to working face-to-face with their clients are sometimes apprehensive about expanding their coaching offering online. Implementing new technologies involves important challenges for creating coaching contents, for training coaches to adapt their practices to technology, and for controlling the quality of the coaching interaction and avoiding ethical risk. Whilst coaching services making use of technology have been proliferating over the years, surprisingly little is known about these practical challenges that coaches working with technology may be coping with, about their experiences with diverse technological tools, or about best practices to optimize digital coaching services. To support successful digital coaching processes, it is useful to first establish the issues that the practitioner faces, and to understand how to cope with the challenges that are inherent in this form of coaching.

Thus, digital coaching needs to be better understood, first by coaching practitioners and then by coaching clients, if we are to embrace it and take full advantage of its potential. Digitalizing the coaching process, or aspects of it, raises several questions:

- How might new media shape the coaching experience? What potential do different technological tools offer? What potential do new technologies promise? What might be the potential threats that technologies bring and how can we cope? What exactly changes when the coaching process takes place remotely in a virtual space?
- How does the coach cope with the issues and challenges that might arise in a digital coaching context? How might the coach compensate for the loss of sensory information and adapt practice to optimize the digital coaching experience? How do we ensure that the quality of digital coaching practice isn't compromised only for the sake of flexibility, time, and cost efficiency?

This book explores these questions, focusing on the digital coach: The human coach who utilizes digital tools to facilitate, to enrich, and to complement the coaching conversation. It explores the meaning of media in the coaching process, it considers how different media alter the quality of the coaching experience, and how the coach might adapt to mediated coaching practice. The book also explores the diversity of media that can be implemented to support coaching processes, it considers the developments that have been made in the digital coaching arena so far, and it anticipates future developments.

The insights offered in the book can be readily used in coaching practice and supervision and they may also be useful for coaches who haven't yet, but are considering to integrate technology in their practice, or are just beginning to do so. They can also be useful to buyers of coaching services, human resource professionals, and software designers. Throughout the book, several case examples are offered to illustrate how coaches make use of different media to enhance the coaching process. The book is based on, and makes extensive reference to the findings of a recent comprehensive, exploratory research study, which inquired into coaches' experiences with digital coaching, and which invited multiple and international perspectives to weigh in. Box 0.1 describes in detail how the study was carried out.

BOX 0.1 AN EXPLORATORY STUDY TO UNDERSTAND COACHES' EXPERIENCES WITH DIGITAL COACHING

Given the increasing spectrum of technologies entering the coaching scene, I conducted a study to explore coaches' practical experiences with these technologies and the challenges they may be facing. I decided to focus on the coach's perspective as I felt that the quality of digital coaching depends a lot on how the practitioner copes with the challenges added by technology and with the lack of physical co-presence with the client. I felt that if digital coaching practice is to be optimized, revealing and analysing the experiences of practicing coaches is key.

I began my research by purposefully selecting a sample of coaches working with technology from the professional online networking platform, LinkedIn. I contacted them individually and asked them about whether they use technology to facilitate their coaching. Following a positive response, I invited them to become members of an online community on the LinkedIn platform, which I had created with the purpose of facilitating knowledge exchanges among participants around digital coaching. The online community allowed me to sustain ongoing, informal dialogue with the participants and to immerse myself in the community's discussions for two years, during which, a total of 1,000 coaches (63% females and 37% males) participated. Participants differed as to the type of coaching they practiced, ranging from life, career, business, leadership, and executive coaching. Using an online community as a source of data collection was a way to allow multiple perspectives to emerge from across the globe. The community sample represented 61 different countries worldwide among which, the UK, USA, and Germany together accounted for 52.3% of the sample. Collecting data through online discussions was also convenient for engaging participants across different time zones without any travel time and costs involved.

My role as a researcher was to facilitate dialogue between the community members and to help the community manage the knowledge and information that its participants shared by regularly summarizing their shared insights and posting these summaries to the community forum. Throughout the process, I asked prompting questions to stimulate discussion and to encourage participants to describe their experiences and to reflect on their practice. By bouncing ideas off one another and exchanging experiences in a community setting, I hoped that participants would surface prominent issues, relevant to their practice and best practices for working around challenges.

I monitored the online community's asynchronous text-based discussions and collected data for this study over a period of two years.[1] I familiarized myself with the data and I identified emerging themes. During my familiarization with the data, I selected members of the community with several years' experience of digital coaching to participate in a one-time, individual, semi-structured telephone interview. The themes that had thus far emerged from the online discussions were used as a basis for the interview guide to the semi-structured telephone interviews that I conducted with 17 selected participants of the community (12 female and 5 male interviewees). The interview data were transcribed, and both data sets (telephone interviews and online discussions) were entered into the qualitative analysis software, MAXQDA. To analyse the data, I followed Mayring's procedural model of qualitative content analysis (2014, p. 80), using inductive reasoning. Data analysis was carried out in an iterative mode, by using inductive category development. The stability of the categories was tested through an intra-coder test on a small portion of the data. An inter-coder comparison was also performed, which allowed the researcher to be once again confronted with the data, to reflect on her reasoning for interpreting the texts and to gain the perspective of a second coder's interpretation. An overview of the study's design is presented in Figure 0.1.

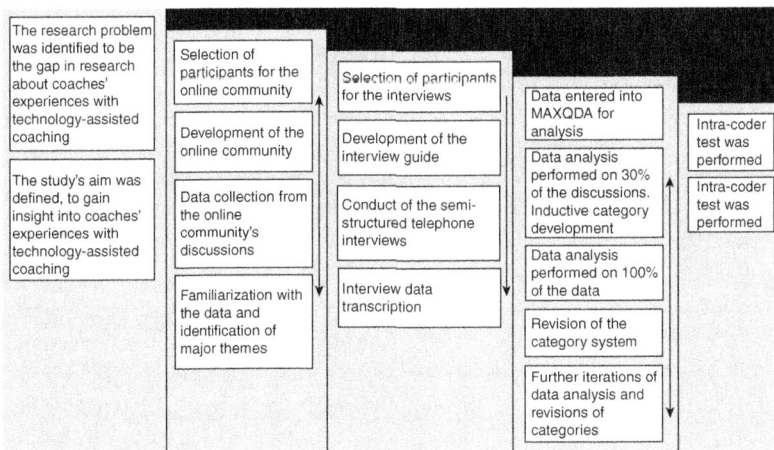

FIGURE 0.1   Research design

My study unveiled coaches' multiple and international perspectives on the phenomenon, allowed to map some of the current developments in the field, and brought to light coaches' experiences with a range of technologies, providing valuable insights into the issues that practitioners are faced with in this form of coaching. These insights will be presented and discussed in this book.

Step 1	Problem identification
Step 2	Clarification of study purpose
Step 3	Selection of a purposive sample of coaches to participate in the online community
Step 4	Development of the online coaching community
Step 5	Data collection from the online community's discussions
Step 6	Familiarization with the data and identification of themes in the data
Step 7	Selection of interview participants
Step 8	Development of the interview guide
Step 9	Conduct of the semi-structured telephone interviews
Step 10	Interview data transcription
Step 11	All data were entered into the software, MAXQDA for analysis
Step 12	Pilot phase of data analysis performed on 30% of the discussions and category development
Step 13	Data analysis performed on 100% of the data and revision of the category system
Step 14	Further iterations of the data analysis were performed, leading to small revisions
Step 15	An intra-coder test was performed
Step 16	An inter-coder test was performed

The study also suffered several limitations: Firstly, it should be acknowledged that having employed a non-probability sampling technique has an impact on the generalizability of this study's findings. A different researcher using a purposive sample might have selected participants based on different criteria. Secondly, the methods that were used to collect the data – the asynchronous online group discussions and the semi-structured telephone interviews – may have also influenced the findings. Past literature has indicated numerous factors that potentially inhibit communication in online communities, among which, the lack of trust and honesty between participants (Borthick & Jones, 2000; Chen et al., 2010; Deris, Koon, & Salam, 2015; Fontainha & Gannon-Leary, 2008), fear of criticism, 'losing face' and misleading others (Ardichvili, Page, & Wentling, 2003), and cross-cultural differences (Ardichvili et al., 2006; LeBaron, Pulkkinen, & Scollin, 2000). Thirdly, as the findings were derived from a worldwide community in the present study, they may have been influenced by cross-cultural differences between participants. Past literature found that cultural heterogeneity affects knowledge sharing in online communities (Ardichvili et al., 2006; Dubé, Bourhis, & Jacob, 2006; LeBaron, Pulkkinen, & Scollin, 2000), and may lead to misinterpretations, and lack of trust between members (Dubé, Bourhis, & Jacob, 2006; Wenger,

McDermott, & Snyder, 2002). A further limitation of collecting data from online group discussions is the uneven contribution of participants' shared insights. As compared to individual interviews, group discussions involve different extents of sharing information for each participant. Dubé, Bourhis, and Jacob (2006) emphasized that within large communities, some members may choose to 'free ride', being passive recipients of the community's shared resources rather than active participants. The study suffered further limitations in terms of the data analysis technique and the interpretation of the findings. The data analysis depended upon the researcher's subjective interpretation and her ability and skill to make insightful judgements. Even though the researcher performed several iterations of data analysis and revisited the category system several times to improve the stability of the categories as recommended by Mayring (2014), the findings of this study emanated from a set of data that was subjectively interpreted by the researcher and may thus, involve bias and potential distortions.

Source: Kanatouri, S. (2018). *Mapping the technology-assisted coaching field through the lens of an online community: An exploratory study.* Doctoral dissertation, Helmut-Schmidt University, University of the Federal Armed Forces, Hamburg.

How the book is structured

The book is organized into five chapters. Chapter 1 explores the meaning of digital coaching, and it distinguishes between its various forms. The chapter provides a context for the book, as it begins by discussing the value of coaching in general, and then goes on to describe the value adds of digital coaching. It proposes that as technology is inevitably incorporated in many coaching practices, there is a need to understand how digital coaching can become more than just a flexible and convenient form of coaching, but a viable and truly helpful approach for the coaching client.

Chapter 2 analyses different communication media and how these media might be used to facilitate the coaching conversation. Different types of media, supporting different communication cues are examined, particularly, audio, auditory-visual, virtual environments, and text. The question this chapter addresses is, which factors should be taken into account by the coaching pair, when selecting a medium for the coaching communication? How does the coaching experience change by using different media?

Chapter 3 offers an orientation to the coach of the different types of digital tools available. Digital tools are differentiated from the media discussed in Chapter 2, in that tools refer to supporting media used to enhance coaching and not only to facilitate the coaching conversation. Some of these tools integrate coaching methods and expertise, and they have been designed specifically for coaching. The chapter maps the landscape of generic and coaching-specific tools, and it explores their features and capabilities. It proposes a taxonomy of tools for the practitioner to make sense of the diversity of tools and it offers suggestions for improving the usability of coaching software.

Chapter 4 reflects on how emerging technologies could play a role in coaching. It explores the potential of immersive Virtual Reality (VR) and Augmented Reality (AR) for coaching practice, by considering the inherent qualities of these technologies and the various use cases of VR/AR in other areas, particularly in training and therapy. Suggestions are offered for how specific VR/AR applications could be used to enhance coaching processes. The chapter goes on to discuss the developments in Artificial Intelligence and how these developments might play a role in coaching practice now and in the future.

While Chapters 2, 3, and 4 focus on the fixed capabilities of media and their role in the coaching process, the focus of Chapter 5 turns to the coach. It asks, 'who is the digital coach?' and examines the practitioner's role in adapting to the capabilities of the medium in use. How does familiarity with a digital tool change the coach's experience? Is it only the media capabilities influencing the coaching experience, or is it the coaching skill and the extent to which, coaching skills have been developed for coaching specifically? The chapter seeks to explore the connection between media capabilities and coaching skill in a digital coaching context, and it approaches digital coaching as a distinct concept from traditional, presence coaching.

Note

1 The online community 'E-coaching: A dialogue between researchers and practitioners' still exists after having completed the research. It can be accessed on LinkedIn at: www.linkedin.com/groups/4553351/.

References

Ardichvili, A., Maurer, M., Li, W., Wentling, T., & Stuedemann, R. (2006). Cultural influences on knowledge sharing through online communities of practice. *Journal of Knowledge Management*, 10 (1), 94–107.

Ardichvili, A., Page, V., & Wentling, T. (2003). Motivation and barriers to participation in virtual knowledge-sharing communities of practice. *Journal of Knowledge Management*, 7 (1), 64–77.

Borthick, F. A. & Jones, R. (2000). The motivation for collaborative discovery learning online and its application in an information systems assurance course. *Issues in Accounting Education*, 15 (2), 181–210.

Chen, P. G., Diaz, N., Lucas, G., & Rosenthal, M. S. (2010). Dissemination of results in community-based participatory research. *American Journal of Preventive Medicine*, 39 (4), 372–378.

Deris, F. D., Koon, R. T. H., & Salam, A. R. (2015). Virtual communities in an online english language learning forum. *International Education Studies*, 8 (13), 79–87.

Dubé, L., Bourhis, A., & Jacob, R. (2006). Towards a typology of virtual communities of practice. *Interdisciplinary Journal of Information, Knowledge and Management*, 1 69–93.

Fontainha, E. & Gannon-Leary, P. (2008). *Communities of practice and virtual learning communities: Benefits, barriers, and success factors.* European Commission Education and Culture DG, Munich Personal RePEc Archive. Retrieved from: https://mpra.ub.uni-muenchen.de/8708/1/MPRA_paper_8708.pdf.

Kanatouri, S. (2018). *Mapping the technology-assisted coaching field through the lens of an online community: An exploratory study.* Unpublished dissertation, Helmut-Schmidt University, University of the Federal Armed Forces, Hamburg.

LeBaron, J., Pulkkinen, J., & Scollin, P. (2000). Problems of student communication in a cross-cultural, international internet course setting. In J. Bourdeau & R. Heller (Eds.), *Proceedings of EdMedia: World conference on educational media and technology 2000* (pp. 558–563). Montreal, Canada: Association for the Advancement of Computing in Education (AACE).

Mayring, P. (Ed.) (2014). *Qualitative content analysis: Theoretical foundation, basic procedures and software solution.* Klagenfurt: Gesis, Leibniz Institut für Sozialwissenschaften / SSOAR, Open Access Repository. n.p.

Wenger, E., McDermott, R., & Snyder, W. M. (Eds.) (2002). *Cultivating communities of practice: A guide to managing knowledge.* Boston, MA: Harvard Business School Press.

1

WHY DIGITAL COACHING?

Coaching as a valuable approach to human development

When people hear the term 'digital coaching' they typically ask two questions: Does it mean coaching without a coach? And does it work? Digital coaching means that coaching is assisted by digital media. Digital media can conveniently facilitate the dialogue between coach and client at a distance, or they may support clients' reflection and problem-solving processes in a self-coaching mode. But, before going into detail about the meaning of digitalizing coaching and whether this mode of coaching could successfully support clients in solving their problems and attaining their goals, it is important to examine why we need coaching in the first place.

Coaching enjoys growing recognition as an approach that can effectively support individuals' and groups' positive change and development in the contexts of work, career, or personal life. It offers 'an intensive and systematic support to outcome-oriented reflection over problems and self-reflection, as well as consultation of individuals or groups to approach self-congruent goals or for conscious self-change and self-development' (Greif, 2008, p. 59 free translation from the original text). The role of the coach is that of a 'process consultant' (Schein, 1999), who facilitates the client's reflection and problem-solving process (Geißler, 2017) and engages with the client in joint exploration of the problem and action planning (Schein, 1999). Greif, Schmidt, and Thamm (2010) suggest that coaching tends to be successful when:

- The coach provides emotional support and shows empathy.
- The coach helps the client set SMART goals (specific, measurable, achievable, realistic, and time-bound).
- The coach guides the client to identify concrete solutions to the problem.

- The coach supports the client's internal and external resource activation.
- The coach supports the client's learning transfer into practice.
- Feedback about the client's satisfaction with the process and post-action evaluation of progress.

The emphasis is thus, on accompanying the client, guiding and facilitating the client's reflection, rather than giving instruction. As such, coaching is distinguished from expert consultation, in which the consultant is commissioned to diagnose the client's problem and to suggest a solution. The coach doesn't have a set curriculum and doesn't determine the coaching contents. Like in psychotherapy, the coach may use methods, such as active listening, reflexive question techniques, mirroring, role-play. It can cover diverse topics, among other, personal life issues, career issues, leadership, work-life balance, performance improvement, work satisfaction, relationship issues, and development of competencies, and it can be offered to individuals or to groups. Whilst coaching has been strongly influenced by the psychotherapeutic tradition (Lee, 2010; Western, 2016) and the two disciplines display some commonalities, for instance in that they provide the client space for self-reflection (Greif, Möller, & Scholl, 2016), coaching differs of course, from psychotherapy, as it focuses on individuals with no identifiable mental health issues.

When coaching emerged in the corporate world in the 1980s, it was a fundamental innovation, as it offered a new method for developing human resources, which until then had relied only on training and teaching (Geißler, 2013). Since the emergence of the field, when coaching was only offered to top management, coaching services have expanded to address all organizational levels as well as non-corporate target groups, and to offer diverse forms of coaching delivery to individuals and groups through face-to-face and technology-assisted communication modalities. Coaching has increasingly gained popularity (Cox, Bachkirova, & Clutterbuck, 2010; Grant, 2003; Grant & Cavanagh, 2007), and research focusing on coaching processes and their outcomes has also seen a steady increase over the years. Industry reports (Bresser, 2013; ICF, 2012) evidence the increase of coaching services, and experts (a.o. Bresser & Wilson, 2006; Bueno, 2010) suggest that coaching is a rapidly growing industry.

Given today's technological and socio-economic drivers of change, the accelerated use of coaching and its expansion across diverse types of clients and contexts are not surprising (see Figure 1.1). With knowledge being valued as a powerful resource, the continuous learning and skill development of individuals become mandatory. Globalization, the Third Industrial Revolution, the rapid pace of technological change, and the vast amount of information available on the internet are correlating with the rapid obsolescence of knowledge, changing skills profiles, and the eclipse of lifetime careers (OECD, 2004; UNESCO, 2005; World Economic Forum, 2018). The knowledge society is closely linked with the advances in technology, particularly the internet, as up-to-date knowledge relies upon the rapid distribution of knowledge through digital media. Moreover, the explosive growth of digital technologies and along with this, the enabled

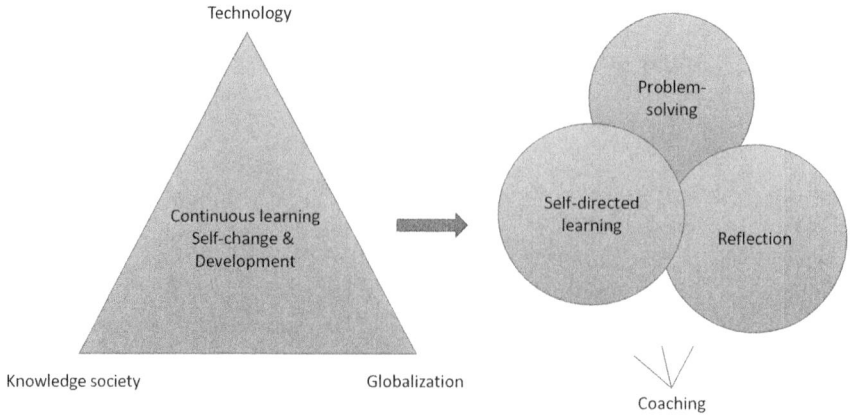

FIGURE 1.1 Coaching for learning, self-change, and self-development

communication and work across geographical borders and time zones have been essential for globalization. Globalization has created enormous pressures for organizations performing in global contexts to be agile in their learning, if they are to stay competitive. The implication of these pressures is that workers are expected to acquire skills rapidly, to adapt to continuously changing conditions, to problem-solve and to be self-directed learners, in order to keep abreast of current knowledge. The instability of skills and the need for workers to upskill or to reskill are expected to become even more pronounced as the Fourth Industrial Revolution is likely to bring about the displacement of some jobs and to create new occupations (World Economic Forum, 2018). In such times of rapid change, self-directed and lifelong learning are critical. The need for continuous learning emphasizes the importance of developing problem-solving skills, and the ability to reflect on oneself, on one's own learning progress, and on the problem at hand. Accompanying individuals and groups in their reflection processes, helping them to solve their own problems and develop, in other words, helping them help themselves (Geißler, 2013) lie at the heart of coaching.

Adding the technology element: what is 'digital coaching'?

Technology can be an enhancement to the increasingly important coaching services. Whilst coaching has traditionally been delivered face-to-face, technological media enable coaching via distance. Technology may be used to facilitate the coaching conversation, but also to enrich the coaching process beyond the coaching dialogue and to enable self-coaching processes. The incorporation of technology in coaching practice has been driven by the need for time savings, cost efficiency, and flexibility in coaching delivery (Kanatouri & Geißler 2016; Kanatouri, 2017). Particularly, as the scope of coaching expanded to include clients representing top management, middle and lower levels of management, as well as employees, groups and teams, the need arose to keep coaching costs down (Kanatouri & Geißler, 2016). Having to cope with the challenge of offering coaching support to more individuals, while at the same time managing the budget for it, led to initiatives that partly or entirely replaced face-to-face coaching with technology-assisted coaching. Table 1.1 summarizes the different possible uses of technology in coaching along with examples.

These different ways of using technology create the following distinct forms of digital coaching:

- *Remote coaching* (relational): Face-to-face communication is entirely replaced with technology-mediated communication, enabling coaching at a distance regardless of geographic location. Examples include telephone, synchronous and asynchronous text-based communication, video calls, HD videoconferencing, and avatar-based coaching. Remote coaching can be coach-led, where communication takes place between a human coach and client. Several interpersonal communication media – telephone and videoconferencing, emails – also enable coaching conversations in a group or team. Interpersonal communication media are discussed in Chapter 2.

- *Remote coaching with supporting tools*: This form of coaching refers to the combined use of remote coaching using one, or more of the above communication media and one or more digital supporting tools during or in between sessions to enhance the coaching process. One example of this form of coaching is using the telephone to facilitate the coaching dialogue in combination with an online journaling tool (supporting tool) for the client to write reflections in between coaching sessions. There is a growing spectrum of possibilities as to how remote coaching can be enriched with such tools. Supporting tools are discussed in Chapter 3 in detail.

- *Blended coaching*: This could be the preferred mode of coaching for many coaches and clients, as it combines the possibility to quickly establish rapport with the client in a face-to-face session, whilst it also allows flexible, time and location independent remote coaching. It involves the combined use of remote and face-to-face coaching sessions, or the integration of digital media in face-to-face coaching sessions. It can take the following different forms:

  o Alternating remote with face-to-face coaching sessions, facilitated by a human coach. For instance, having remote sessions as follow-ups to face-to-face coaching sessions or after an initial face-to-face session and closing with a last face-to-face session.
  o Face-to-face coaching sessions combined with computer-based supporting tools or with self-coaching programs.

- *Self-coaching*: Desktop-based or mobile self-coaching applications, without facilitation by a human coach, typically involve a series of questions to take

TABLE 1.1 Digital coaching modalities

	Audio-only	Audio-visual	Text	Visual
Coach–client dialogue	• Phone • Asynchronous audio messages	• Video calls • HD videoconferencing • Avatar worlds with built-in audio (or text) chat • Asynchronous video messages	• Email • Synchronous/ asynchronous text-chat	–
Complementary support to the coach–client dialogue	• Audio podcasts	• Videos • Vlogs	• Blogs • Online articles • Pre-set question sets • Journals	• Images • Online constellations • Virtual worlds
Machine–client interaction			• Pre-set question frameworks • Coaching chatbots	–

coachees from reflecting on a problem and setting goals, to identifying and activating their resources, to creating an action plan for reaching their goal. We are increasingly seeing AI-assisted coaching apps, and such apps are very likely to increase in the future, as AI becomes more powerful and fed with large data sets. Currently, most self-coaching programs offer the option to follow up with a human coach, in a blended form of coaching, whilst there are also some, that are intended as standalone short coaching programs. Even though the functionality or depth of self-coaching programs is currently rather limited, we are likely to observe a changing landscape of self-coaching apps in the future, particularly as AI becomes more intelligent. Self-coaching may be regarded now as the inadequate alternative to relational coaching, quick, cheap, and inefficient. It will take a long time to shake off suspicions around it, but eventually, as AI is fed with theoretical coaching models and with more data, it could become effective for addressing at least simple coaching issues.

The forms of digital coaching discussed above are depicted in Figure 1.2.
Thus, digital coaching may involve any of the following options:

1. *With* versus *without facilitation by a human coach:*

   a) When a human coach is involved, technology can be used to enable the coach–client communication at a distance. These range from telephone and video calls, to synchronous and asynchronous text-chat, and HD videoconferencing.

   b) Without facilitation by a human coach, a machine–client interaction is involved in a self-coaching process. Clients may for instance, have a dialogue with a chatbot or they may be guided by pre-structured coaching questions and other resources to attain their coaching goals.

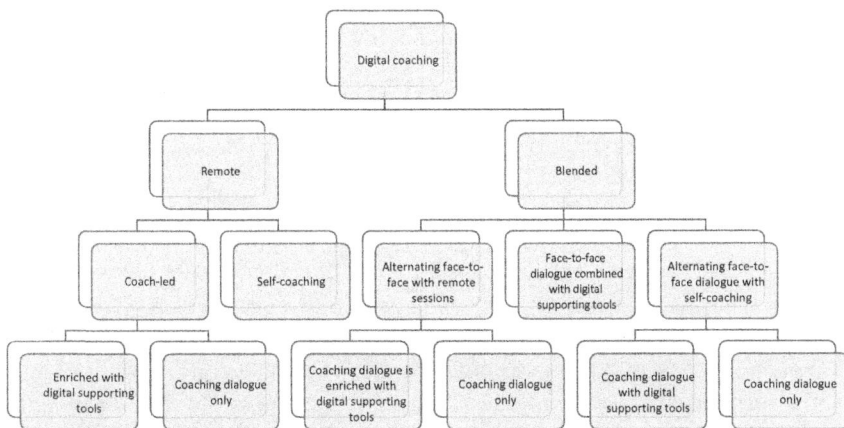

FIGURE 1.2 Forms of digital coaching

2. Supporting the *entire coaching process* versus *parts of the coaching process:*

    a) Media can be used to support clients throughout the entire coaching process. They accompany clients from reflecting on a problem, identifying goals, developing action plans, through to transfer to practice and evaluating the process after taking action.

    b) Alternatively, media may assist with only certain aspects of coaching, such as for instance, with setting goals and developing an action plan.

3. *Facilitating* the (individual or group) coaching conversation (or self-coaching process) versus *complementing* the (individual or group) coaching conversation:

    a) Media may be used to facilitate the communication between coach and client or self-coaching process. These include communication media, such as audio and video calls, synchronous and asynchronous text-chat, chatbots, and predefined sets of self-coaching questions.

    b) Media can be used to complement and to augment the coaching process by supporting clients' reflection and problem-solving beyond the coaching dialogue. They may be used between coaching sessions to encourage clients' reflection and to provide the coach feedback about clients' progress. They may also be used during the coaching conversation, for example, to structure and to document the conversation, or to visualize relationships. Examples include pre-structured written question sets, journals, images, graphs, and simulations.

A second-best solution?

One might easily assume that in a helping relationship such as coaching, building rapport and trust, providing emotional support and showing empathy, tuning in and being attentive to clients may be best achieved through face-to-face contact and physical proximity. Such an assumption is justifiable, as face-to-face contact allows us to use all five senses to connect to the other person, using both verbal and non-verbal cues to communicate. After all, face-to-face communication is what we are most used to.

And yet, the continuously evolving communication media and the widespread use of computer-based communications suggest that we *can* connect, work, and learn at a physical distance from one another, with or without face-to-face contact, real-time or asynchronously. Over time, as we leverage the possibilities of technology, we become increasingly accustomed to, and comfortable with using technology in our professional and personal environments. Even when handling personal or sensitive information, technology provides alternative channels to face-to-face communication that allow us to exchange sensitive data and to give emotional support. Crisis hotlines, such as the Samaritans have used the telephone for over 65 years to deliver psychological support, and later added email and instant messaging to their services (Pollock et al., 2010).

The telephone has also been one of the first communication technologies to be used for coaching purposes (Boyce & Clutterbuck, 2011) and later, text-based communication media and video calls were incorporated into coaching practice as well (ICF, 2007; Sherpa, 2008, 2012, 2015, 2017). Even though empirical coaching research is scarce, there is some empirical evidence to suggest the efficacy of coaching via telephone and computer-based communication, and to demonstrate the suitability of these media for building trusting relationships between coach and client (Berry, 2005; Geißler et al., 2014; Ghods, 2009; Hancock, 2014; McLaughlin, 2012; Poepsel, 2011; Ribbers & Warringa, 2015) and for leading to positive coaching outcomes and client satisfaction (Ghods, 2009; Poepsel, 2011). Table 1.2 lists 17 empirical coaching studies that examined the use of different media in coaching and generally indicated coaches' and/or clients' positive experiences.

The focus of the coaching studies in Table 1.2 has been mainly in examining telephone and text-based interactions. Insights into experiences with newer technologies, such as virtual worlds, but also with technology-mediated communication in team coaching and in supervision are still very limited.

The available studies, while offering mainly positive findings about coaches' and coaching clients' experiences with the media under investigation, they examined different aspects of the technology-assisted coaching experience and they suffered methodological limitations, which prevent from drawing firm conclusions about the effectiveness of digital coaching.

The more established psychological and psychotherapeutic literatures lend some support to coaching research, as they evidence the feasibility of both online and telephone-based therapeutic interventions and indicate that they can be equally efficacious to face-to-face interventions (a.o. Barak et al., 2008; Cook & Doyle, 2002; Lovell et al., 2007; Ludman et al., 2007; Mohr et al., 2012; Murphy, Mitchell, & Hallett, 2011; Reese, Conoley, & Brossart, 2002; Simon et al., 2004). Table 1.3 presents examples of these studies.

The increasing role of technology in coaching

Given the strong influence of technology in all aspects of our life and the, albeit limited, evidence that digital coaching could be a viable mode of coaching, it is no surprise that technology is increasingly used to support coaching practice. Market reports evidence this increase: Already in 2007, the International Coach Federation (ICF)'s global survey indicated that 50% of a sample of 7,000 coaches delivered coaching mainly over distance, particularly via telephone (ICF, 2007). Since then, market research has observed an increase in delivering coaching at a distance and an increased use of richer communication media (specifically, video calls and HD videoconferencing). Between 2012 and 2019, the Sherpa Executive Coaching Survey reported a decrease in face-to-face coaching (from 41% to 32%) and an increase in coaching via distance (from 59% to 68%) (See Figure 1.3).

More specifically, between 2012 and 2019 the Sherpa Executive Coaching Survey found that:

TABLE 1.2 Overview of digital coaching studies

Date	Researcher(s)	Design	Technologies investigated	Study aims/variables tested	Findings
2002	Charbonneau, M. A.	Qualitative	Phone	Factors influencing coaches' and clients' media choices	Despite a preference for face-to-face over telephone coaching, the success of technology-assisted coaching was found to be related to the fit between the coach and their preferred medium, between the client and their preferred medium, and a good fit between coach and client
2005	Berry, R. M.	Quantitative	Phone	Clients' satisfaction with coaching relationship and coaching outcomes	Telephone coaching was found to be a comparable solution to face-to-face coaching, in terms of rapport building and coaching outcomes
2007	Geißler, H., Helm, M., Nolze, A.	Qualitative	Coaching-specific software (text-based)	Satisfaction with online self-coaching for different target groups and different coaching issues	Findings showed participants were very satisfied with the online self-coaching tool, but they wished for additional support via telephone with a personal coach
2008	Frazee, R. V.	Mixed methods	Phone, Skype video, email, file sharing	Extent and factors affecting the use of technology-assisted coaching in organizations from the perspectives of coaches and learning professionals	The results suggested coaches' preference for face-to-face coaching, and for leaner media, such as email compared to richer media, such as videoconferencing. The study highlighted the usefulness of technology in coaching and predicted its increased use in the future
2009	Ghods, N.	Quantitative	Phone	Coaching relationship and outcomes as perceived by clients and their observers	Telephone coaching can facilitate strong coaching relationships and it can bring about positive and sustainable coaching outcomes, as perceived by coachees, their supervisors and peers

Year	Author	Research design	Technology	Aim/Focus	Findings
2011	Poepsel, M.	Quantitative	Coaching-specific software (text-based)	Clients' hope, subjective well-being, goal attainment	Participation in the online coaching program that was developed for this study encouraged participants' reflection and it increased their subjective goal attainment and well-being
2012	McLaughlin, M.	Qualitative	Phone	Coaches' experiences with telephone coaching	Telephone coaching differs from face-to-face coaching, as it requires an adaptation of coaches' skills. Telephone is a comparable medium to face-to-face coaching, if not a more powerful medium for coaching, which can facilitate rapport and trust building
2012	Geißler, H., Metz, M. Kurzmann, C.	Qualitative	Phone and coaching-specific software (text-based)	Telephone coaching enriched with text-based tools and online counselling, as compared to face-to-face processes	The use of text-based tools in combination with telephone coaching could potentially offer similar support to that provided by face-to-face coaching
2013	Jones, C.	Mixed methods	Skype video	To explore coachees' experiences with Skype coaching in comparison to face-to-face coaching	Skype coaching was perceived by participants to provide a similar experience to face-to-face coaching
2013	Taranovych, Y.	Qualitative	Coaching-specific software (text-based)	Requirements, design, implementation and evaluation of a web-based system for project management coaching	Participants evaluated the online platform positively and the platform was perceived useful for coaching for project management
2014	Hancock, B.	Qualitative	Skype and coaching-specific	Clients' experiences with the coaching program	The study demonstrated clients' positive evaluations of the combined use of Skype and the text-based tool, and it provided insights into the skills and

(Continued)

TABLE 1.2 (Cont.)

Date	Researcher(s)	Design	Technologies investigated	Study aims/variables tested	Findings
			software (text-based)		competencies that are critical for delivering coaching remotely, as perceived by coaches in the study
2014	Andrews, A.	Qualitative	Second Life® (virtual world)	Clients' experiences with Second Life® coaching	The findings revealed mixed reactions to the virtual world coaching experience, although they generally showed that Second Life® could be a feasible technology for delivering coaching
2014	Geißler, H. Hasenbein, M. Kanatouri, S. Wegener, R.	Mixed methods	Phone and coaching-specific software (text-based)	Clients' satisfaction with the coaching program and goal attainment	The combination of text-based questions with telephone conversation was successful in facilitating effective coaching interventions in terms of clients' perceived goal attainment
2014	Ribbers, A. Warringa, A.	Mixed methods	Coaching-specific software (text-based)	Clients' evaluation of web-based coaching program effectiveness in improving their managerial skills	The study's findings were positive, suggesting the effectiveness of online coaching for improving managers' skills
2017	Deniers, C.	Qualitative	Skype video	Clients' experience with Skype video coaching	The study highlighted clients' perceived strengths as well as weaknesses of Skype coaching
2018	Kanatouri, S.	Qualitative	Generic communication media and coaching-specific software	Coaches' experience with the use of technology in coaching	Digital coaching differs from face-to-face coaching and it requires an adaptation of skills. Challenges with digital coaching may be surmountable through skill development

| 2019 | Woods, N. | Mixed methods | Current technologies (audio, video, text-based communication media) and emerging technologies (incl. virtual and augmented reality, AI, blockchain) | Coaches' opinions and attitudes about the use of high-tech solutions in coaching | Technology was used to supplement and/or replace face-to-face coaching, as well as for coach selection, process management and evaluation. Technology was perceived to offer value throughout the coaching process, and it was predicted that it will continue to do so in the future |

TABLE 1.3 Overview of technology-assisted counselling and psychotherapeutic studies

Date	Researcher(s)	Design	Technologies investigated	Study aims/variables tested	Findings
2002	Cook & Doyle	Quantitative	Asynchronous and synchronous text-chat	Patients' evaluation of their online therapeutic relationship	The study indicated the efficacy of online therapy in terms of the relationship between therapist and patient (working alliance), as perceived by patients. The telephone was perceived to have a disinhibition effect
2002	Reese, Conoley, & Brossart	Quantitative	Telephone	The effectiveness of telephone counselling, from clients' perspectives, in terms of the process and outcomes, and their evaluation of their counselling relationship	Telephone counselling was perceived to be an effective intervention, as indicated by participants' self-reports. The findings showed participants' positive relationship self-ratings and satisfaction with telephone counselling
2004	Simon et al.	Quantitative	Telephone	Measured patient-rated improvement and satisfaction in three therapy conditions to treat depression: face-to-face, face-to-face care with three telephone-based sessions, and face-to-face with a program of eight telephone therapy sessions	Compared to face-to-face treatment, telephone-based therapy led to lower depression scores
2006	Lovell et al.	Quantitative	Telephone	The effectiveness of telephone-based Cognitive Behavioural Therapy for obsessive compulsive disorder compared to face-to-face treatment	The findings demonstrated that the two modes of providing therapy, telephone and face-to-face, were equivalent in terms of the outcomes at four times of data collection and in terms of participants' satisfaction
2007	Ludman et al.	Quantitative	Telephone	Evaluation of telephone-based Cognitive Behavioural Therapy for depression as compared to face-to-face therapy	Telephone-based treatment was more effective in reducing depression than face-to-face treatment

2008	Barak et al.	Quantitative	Online	A meta-analysis of 92 studies, which examined the effectiveness of online therapy with clients treated for a variety of mentalhealth problems	Online therapy is a viable mode of therapy and equally efficacious to face-to-face interventions
2009	Murphy et al.	Quantitative	Online (asynchronous text)	A survey that examined clients' satisfaction with online counselling as compared to face-to-face counselling	No significant difference between online and face-to-face counselling
2012	Mohr et al.	Quantitative	Telephone	The efficacy of telephone-based Cognitive Behavioural Therapy compared to face-to-face treatment for major depressive disorder	Telephone and face-to-face treatments were equally effective at the end of the intervention. However, face-to-face treatment was significantly superior to telephone treatment after a six-month period

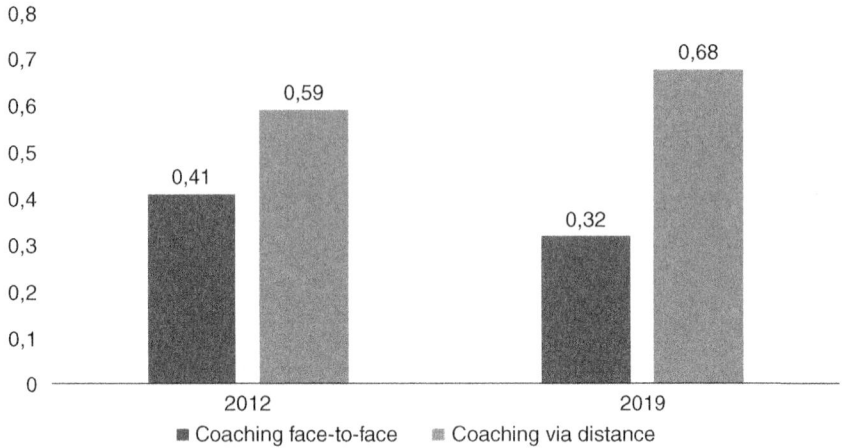

FIGURE 1.3 The increase in distance coaching (2012–2019)

(*Sources*: Diagram created by the author based on the results of the Sherpa Executive Coaching Survey Reports 2012 and 2019)

- The use of telephone remained stable (25%).
- There was a slight decrease in the use of text-based coaching (from 11% to 8%).
- There was an increased use of video calls (from 15% to 25% in 2019) and in HD videoconferencing (from 4% to 10%) (See Figure 1.4).

These findings suggest that technology and especially video-based communication media are increasingly integrated in coaching practices. The increased use

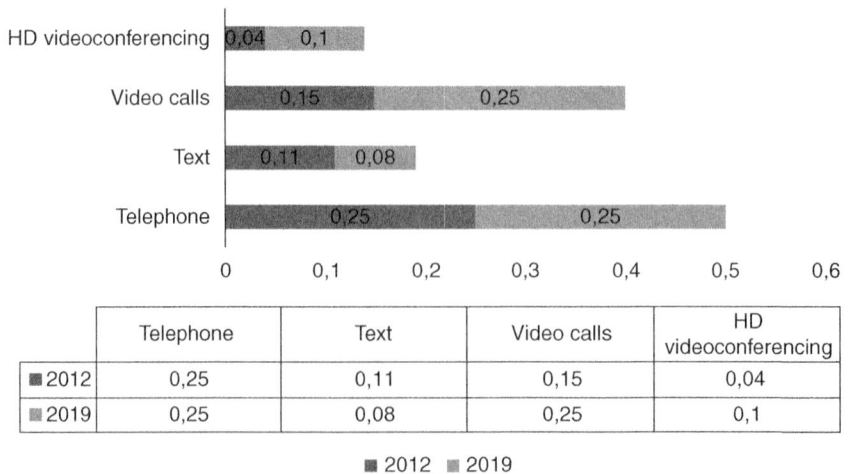

	Telephone	Text	Video calls	HD videoconferencing
∎2012	0,25	0,11	0,15	0,04
∎2019	0,25	0,08	0,25	0,1

∎ 2012 ∎ 2019

FIGURE 1.4 The increase in rich communication media (2012–2019)

(*Sources*: Based on the results of the Sherpa Executive Coaching Survey Reports 2012 and 2019)

of video is justifiable, as it resembles more closely face-to-face communication as compared to audio- and text-based media. Given that the performance of video communication media has improved and continues to improve, video-based coaching is on the rise.

The practical advantages of digital coaching

Technology offers several practical advantages for supporting coaching processes and supervision, for managing procedures such as scheduling sessions and invoicing, for coach selection, and for the reach of coaching to wider audiences. Specifically, digital coaching may offer the following practical advantages:

*   *Time and cost savings:* Coach and client can interact from the convenience of their home, office or other environment, thereby eliminating travel time and reducing cost.
*   *Contact frequency:* The reduced cost involved by not having to travel to get to the client implies that coaching can take place more frequently and it can be sustained for longer periods of time, as compared to coaching face-to-face, or it can bridge the time in between face-to-face coaching sessions. Alternatively, digital media, such as asynchronous/synchronous text-chat, and digital coaching software for writing online journals or for reflecting on predefined coaching questions, can be used to bridge the time in between remote coaching sessions. The convenience of online communication can be used to give clients a sense that their coach is 'there for them' to support them on every step of the way.
*   *Flexibility and convenience:* Without travel, coach and client are more flexible in scheduling sessions at short notice and convenient times for both, regardless of geographic location and time zones. As coaching works out to fit around their schedule, the time barriers are reduced and coaching becomes possible for more people. The coach can keep session notes and manage client data on a secure online space, such as their profile information, aims, agreements, contact information, and invoices.
*   *Accessibility:* Digital coaching becomes accessible to many, as it transcends geographic barriers and it facilitates clients' access to expertise. Clients are not limited to the coach in their area, but they can choose the coach that fits their needs best, for instance in terms of educational background, relevant experience, and years of experience. Organizations can offer coaching to more employees, as the time and cost is much less than face-to-face coaching. Digital coaching also enables coaches' access to more clients, regardless of their location.
*   *Structure:* Verbal communication can be quickly forgotten, or one may get lost if thoughts and ideas are complex and multi-sided. Digital coaching, specifically asynchronous audio- and text-based communication allows time to collect and structure one's thoughts.

- *Innovation:* Digital coaching offers new ways of supporting the client, which are not available in traditional, face-to-face coaching, such as the option to place the client in a virtual world or scenario to visualize a situation, to practice new behaviours and to test potential solutions in a safe environment. The coach and coachee, or team of coachees may collaborate towards a goal in a virtual environment. They may create a virtual place for their team to meet, such as a house within a virtual environment, or they may teleport to an inspiring or peaceful landscape where they can have their meeting, and they can use symbolic objects to convey an idea.

The challenges of digital coaching

Whilst digital coaching offers obvious practical advantages, it can be a challenging mode of practicing, quite likely more challenging than face-to-face coaching. It is important to identify the challenges that may arise during the digital coaching process and to understand how the coach can overcome them. For instance, it's important for the practitioner to understand how to cope with:

- *Technical challenges:* Technical challenges might include disruptions due to breaks in the internet connection, limitations in the capabilities of a software, or complex handling of a tool. The practitioner needs to be able to smoothly integrate technology in coaching, to troubleshoot within a session, to guide the client in using the tool, and to be able, if necessary, to switch to an alternative tool to minimize disruption or a different tool that the client feels comfortable using.
- *The lack of physical presence:* When coaching at a physical distance, for instance via telephone or video communication, the absence of physical co-presence of the coaching pair could create a challenge for observing clients' body language, assessing their emotional states and gaining a complete picture of them. Physical distance between the coaching pair could be more of a barrier, when clients face an emotionally charged situation.
- *Reduced sensory data:* When coaching via telephone or computer-based media, sensory cues are reduced. The coach may rely for instance, on auditory cues in the case of telephone coaching, while missing out on clients' facial expressions, gestures, posture, hand gestures, and physical presence. The coach will rely only on clients' written words when coaching via text, missing out on non-verbal cues, such as clients' tone of voice, pitch, speed of speech, breathing patterns, silences, and body language.
- *Ethical challenges:* Using digital media creates additional risks of a breach of clients' data privacy and confidentiality. There are various reasons for this:
  - When information is being exchanged through electronic means, there is a history of those interactions. The chance of a breach or of some accidental disclosure is higher than a face-to-face coaching conversation, of which there is no record, unless it has been agreed to record it.

- ○ Many organizations monitor email traffic.
- ○ Files may contain viruses and computers can be hacked.
- ○ Non-encrypted platforms like Skype have a low data security.

How do we make it work?

Despite its challenges, digital coaching is an increasingly popular form of coaching. Aside from its practical value, there is at least some empirical evidence to suggest that digital coaching could be a viable alternative, or it might even be an equally viable mode of practice to face-to-face coaching. Given the ubiquity of technology in our lives and working environments, and the convenience it offers, it is not anymore so much a question of *whether* digital media should be used to deliver coaching, but it's about *how* this is done, so that successful coaching outcomes are achieved. It is about becoming aware of the risks and limitations that it introduces and about developing skills and best practices to smoothly integrate technology in coaching practice and to create and sustain coaching relationships at a distance. For the coaching practitioner working with technology, or the prospective digital coach, it is important to understand how coaching methods and techniques translate to digital environments and if there is a digital solution to replace each of the methods and materials that are used in traditional, face-to-face coaching. What is gained and what is lost? What should the coach pay attention to? Can new media even expand the potential of coaching practice? Can some media enrich the coaching process in ways that face-to-face interaction can't? The following chapter addresses some of these questions, and it explores how different communication technologies mediate the coaching conversation at a distance and thereby, alter the coaching experience from the traditional, face-to-face coaching.

References

Barak, A., Hen, L., Boniel-Nissim, M., & Shapira, N. (2008). A comprehensive review and a meta-analysis of the effectiveness of internet-based psychotherapeutic interventions. *Journal of Technology in Human Services*, 26 (2–4), 109–160.

Berry, R. M. (2005). *A comparison of face-to-face and distance coaching practices: The role of the working alliance in problem resolution.* Unpublished doctoral dissertation, Georgia State University, Atlanta, GA.

Boyce, L. A. & Clutterbuck, D. (2011). E-coaching: Accept it, it's here, and it's evolving! In G. Hernez Broome & L. Boyce (Eds.) *Advancing executive coaching: Setting the course for successful leadership coaching* (pp. 285–315). San Francisco, CA: Jossey-Bass.

Bresser, F. (2013). *The state of coaching across the globe: Results of the Global Coaching Survey 2008/2009* (August 2009). Retrieved from: www.dgfp.de/wissen/personalwissen-direkt/dokument/82319/herunterladen.

Bresser, F. & Wilson, C. (2006). What is coaching? In J. Passmore (Ed.), *Excellence in coaching: The industry guide* (1st Edition, pp. 9–25). London / Philadelphia: Kogan Page.

Bueno, J. (2010). Coaching: One of the fastest growing industries in the world. *Therapy Today*, 21 (7), 10–15.

Cook, J. & Doyle, D. (2002). Working alliance in online therapy as compared to face-to-face therapy: Preliminary results. *CyberPsychology and Behavior*, 5 (2), 95–105.

Cox, E., Bachkirova, T., & Clutterbuck, D. (Eds.) (2010). *The Complete handbook of coaching*. London / California / New Delhi / Singapore: Sage.

Geißler, H. (2013). Produktdiversifizierung und Erschließung neuer Marktsegmente durch Coaching mit modernen Medien. In R. Wegener, M. Loebbert, & A. Fritze (Eds.) *Coaching-Praxisfelder: Forschung und Praxis im Dialog* (pp. 260–271). Wiesbaden: Springer.

Geißler, H. (Ed.) (2017). *Die Grammatik des Coachens: Eine Empirische Rekonstruktion*. Wiesbaden: Springer.

Geißler, H., Hasenbein, M., Kanatouri, S., & Wegener, R. (2014). E-coaching: Conceptual and empirical findings of a virtual coaching programme. *International Journal of Evidence Based Coaching and Mentoring*, 12 (2), 165–187.

Ghods, N. (2009). *Distance coaching: The relationship between coach-client relationship, client satisfaction, and coaching outcomes*. Unpublished doctoral dissertation, San Diego University, USA.

Grant, A. M. (2003). The impact of life coaching on goal-attainment, metacognition and mental health. *Social Behaviour and Personality*, 31 (3), 253–264.

Grant, A. M. & Cavanagh, M. J. (2007). Evidence-based coaching: Flourishing or languishing? *Australian Psychologist*, December 2007, 42 (4), 239–254.

Greif, S. (Ed.) (2008). *Coaching und ergebnisorientiere Selbstreflexion* (1st edition). Göttingen: Hogrefe.

Greif, S., Möller, H., & Scholl, W. (2016). Coachingdefinitionen und -konzepte. In S. Greif, H. Möller, & W. Scholl (Eds.), *Handbuch Schlüsselkonzepte für das Coaching* (pp. 1–9). Berlin / Heidelberg: Springer.

Greif, S., Schmidt, F., & Thamm, A. (2010). The rating of eight coaching success factors – Observation manual, Version 4. Work and Organizational Psychology Unit, University of Osnabrück, Germany. Available online at: www.home.uni-osnabrueck.de/sgreif/downloads/Rating_of_Coaching_Success_Factors_Version4-May_2010.pdf.

Hancock, B. (2014). *The design of a framework and instrument for assessment of virtual coaching competence: An exploratory study*. Master's thesis, Stellenbosch University, South Africa.

International Coaching Federation (ICF). (2012). *Global coaching study*. Retrieved from: www.coachfederation.org/files/FileDownloads/2012GlobalCoachingStudy.pdf?_ga=1.154453816.124482212.1424978859.

International Coach Federation (ICF)/PricewaterhouseCoopers. (2007). *Global coaching study: Executive summary*. Revised February 2007. Retrieved from: http://coachfedera tion.org/files/includes/docs/064GlobalCoachingStudyExecutiveSummary2008.pdf.

Kanatouri, S. (2017). The role of online coaching tools in the coaching process: Insights from an online community. *Wirtschaftspsychologie Aktuell: Zeitschrift für Personal und Management*, 2, 16–26.

Kanatouri, S. & Geißler, H. (2016). Adapting to working with new technologies. In T. Bachkirova, G. Spence, & D. Drake (Eds.), *The Sage handbook of coaching* (pp. 715–730). Los Angeles / London / N. Delhi / Singapore / Washington DC / Melbourne: Sage.

Lee, G. (2010). The psychodynamic approach to coaching. In E. Cox, T. Bachkirova, & D. Clutterbuck (Eds.), *The complete handbook of coaching* (pp. 23–36). London / Thousand Oaks / N. Delhi / Singapore: Sage.

Lovell, K., Cox, D., Haddock, G., Jones, C., Raines, D., Garvey, R., Roberts, C., & Hadley, S. (2007). Telephone administered cognitive behaviour therapy for treatment of obsessive compulsive disorder: Randomised controlled non-inferiority trial. *The British Medical Journal*, 333 (7574), 883.

Ludman, E. J., Simon, G. E., Tutty, S., & Von Korff, M. (2007). A randomized trial of telephone psychotherapy and pharmacotherapy for depression: Continuation and durability of effects. *Journal of Consulting and Clinical Psychology*, 75 (2), 257–266.

McLaughlin, M. (2012). *Less is more: The executive coach's experience of working on the telephone.* Unpublished Master's thesis, Oxford Brookes University, UK.

Mohr, D. C., Ho, J., Juffecy, J., Reifler, D., Sokol, L., Burns, M. N., Jin, L., & Siddique, J. (2012). Effect of telephone-administered versus face-to-face cognitive behavioural therapy on adherence to therapy and depression outcomes among primary care patients: A randomized trial. *The Journal of the American Therapy Association*, 307 (21), 2278–2285.

Murphy, L. J., Mitchell, D. L., & Hallett, R. H. (2011). *A comparison of client characteristics in cyber and in-person counselling.* Online resource. Retrieved from: http://therapyonline.ca/cybercounselling/_protected/resources/Readings/Client_Characteristics_in_Cyber_and_In-Person_Counselling.pdf.

OECD. (2004). *Lifelong learning.* Policy Brief February 2004. Paris: OECD.

Poepsel, M. (2011). *The impact of an online evidence-based coaching program on goal striving, subjective well-being, and level of hope.* Doctoral dissertation, Capella University, USA.

Pollock, K., Armstrong, S., Coveney, C., & Moore, J. (2010). *An evaluation of Samaritans telephone and email emotional support service.* NHS National Institute for Health Research and University of Nottingham. Online resource Retrieved from: www.samaritans.org/sites/default/files/kcfinder/files/research/Samaritans_service_evaluation_Nottingham_Full_Report.pdf

Reese, R. J., Conoley, C. W., & Brossart, D. F. (2002). Effectiveness of telephone counselling: A field-based investigation. *Journal of Counselling Psychology*, 49 (2), 233–242.

Ribbers, A. & Warringa, A. (2015). *E-coaching for leadership development.* E-coaching Journal, January 2015. Retrieved from: https://digitalcoach.home.blog/2014/01/15/research-report-about-web-based-coaching-by-anne-ribbers-alexander-warringa/#more-719.

Schein, E. (Ed.) (1999). *Process consultation revisited: Building the helping relationship.* Reading, MA: Addison-Wesley Publishing Inc.

Sherpa Executive Coaching Survey. (2008). *Third annual report.* Retrieved from: www.coachxp.com/docs/SherpaExecutiveCoachingSurvey2008.pdf.

Sherpa Executive Coaching Survey. (2012). *Seventh annual report.* Retrieved from: www.associationforcoaching.com/media/uploads/publications/Survey-Executive-Coaching-2012.pdf.

Sherpa Executive Coaching Survey. (2015). *Tenth annual coaching survey, Public report.* Retrieved from: www.sherpacoaching.com/pdf%20files/2015_Executive_Coaching_Survey_Public-Report.pdf.

Sherpa Executive Coaching Survey. (2017). *Twelfth annual industry review, Public report.* Retrieved from: www.sherpacoaching.com/pdf%20files/2017_Executive_Coaching_Survey_PUBLIC.pdf.

Simon, G. E., Ludman, E. J., Tutty, S., Operskalski, B., & Von Korrf, M. (2004). Telephone psychotherapy and telephone care management for primary care patients starting antidepressant treatment: A randomized controlled trial. *The Journal of the American Therapy Association*, 292 (8), 935–942.

UNESCO. (2005). *Towards knowledge societies: UNESCO World Report.* Paris: UNESCO Publishing. Retrieved from: www.kvab.be/Denkersprogramma/f2ks/UNESCO_Towards_KS.pdf.

Western, S. (2016). The key discourses of coaching. In T. Bachkirova, G. Spence, & D. Drake (Eds.), *The Sage handbook of coaching* (pp. 42–61). Los Angeles / London / N. Delhi / Singapore / Washington DC / Melbourne: Sage.

World Economic Forum. (2018). *The future of jobs report.* Retrieved from: http://reports.weforum.org/future-of-jobs-2016/preface/.

2

THE MEDIATED COACHING DIALOGUE

The coaching conversation: explicit and implicit meanings

As a helping relationship, effective communication between coach and client lies at the heart of coaching. Communication involves the exchanges of explicit and implicit messages (Watzlawick, Beavin, & Jackson, 1967, p. 31). Not only 'what' is said, but also 'how' something is said or written, done or shown shapes interpersonal communication. We use verbal language to communicate with one another, but also non-verbal signals such as the tone of voice, speed of speaking, facial expressions, gestures, body language, and contextual cues, all of which can complement what is being said and facilitate understanding. During the coaching conversation, we exchange straightforward explicit information – for instance, when describing a situation, event, or problem, or in the form of psycho-educative resources to enhance coping skills or to reduce stress – but, also implicit messages, which may reveal our emotions, perceptions, and attitudes, and they may complement or contradict our explicit messages.

Effective communication depends on understanding our communication partner's implicit intention (Searle, 1991) and not only explicit messages. The challenge of course as mentioned before, is that implicit messages convey the speaker's intention, which may or may not match the speaker's explicit message. Austin (1962) made a distinction between locutionary, illocutionary, and perlocutionary speech acts. A locutionary act is an act of saying something through words, whilst an illocutionary act is performed in saying something through which the speaker's intentions are expressed, and a perlocutionary act refers to the effect that is caused by the speech act (Austin, 1962). Illocutionary speech acts, or otherwise referred to as 'indirect speech acts', can be observed in assertions, promises, requests, and expressions of attitudes or emotions, and they can differ from the literal meaning of the words used (Searle, 1975). For example, a client says that she's feeling well, but unintentionally, her body language and tone of voice reveal that she may be troubled and upset. The coach needs to be aware of such conflicting messages and to actively listen to the client's explicit and implicit messages (Clutterbuck et al., 2019).

As implied with the above example, communication doesn't only involve intentionally directed messages. Watzlawick, Beavin, and Jackson (1967) went as far to suggest that 'we cannot not communicate' (pp. 30–32), suggesting that not only intentional message transmission, but every behaviour is communication, even silence and inactivity. On the other hand, physical copresence doesn't necessarily mean that unintentional messages should always be understood as interactional communication. As Seidl (2004) explained:

> every communication refers to the fact that all participants perceive each other as present – a face-to-face contact is thus a precondition. However, not everyone who is physically present will also be treated as present by the communication. For example, people at other tables in a restaurant although physically present might not be considered present by the interactional communication. Similarly, not all perceptible behaviour will necessarily be treated as perceptible, i.e. treated as present, by the interaction; for example, blowing one's nose. In other words, every interactional communication distinguishes between what to consider as present and what to consider as absent. Making this distinction qualifies the communication as interactional. One could also say, the interactional communications carry the code 'presence/absence' analogously to the function codes described above.
>
> *(p. 15)*

As we've seen, to understand the client's emotions, needs, or intentions, the coach needs to be very aware of the client's intentional and unintentional communication messages, and carefully listen to explicit and implicit messages. Even more so, when some sensory cues are absent.

The active role of media in the construction of meaning in the coaching communication

So, what role might media play in the coaching conversation? How do they influence the coach's understanding of clients' intended meaning?

For some scholars (Clark, 1983, 1985; Shannon & Weaver, 1963), media are the means of transmitting (and receiving) communication messages like parcels (Reddy, 1979) and the nature of the medium has no influence on the communication or the learning process. This view assumes that there is no discrepancy between the meaning of the message that is transmitted by the sender and its perception and interpretation when it reaches the receiver. Different media thus, could also lead to similar learning outcomes (Clark, 1994). The receiver passively

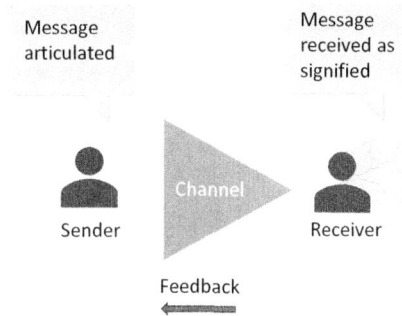

FIGURE 2.1 The transmission communication model

consumes the message as it was transmitted, and regardless of whether the medium accommodates for instance, written, auditory, or audio-visual cues (see Figure 2.1). Implicit meanings, the complexity of human emotions, intentions, and behaviours, and their influence on interpersonal communication processes are however, ignored in this model.

Given the dynamic nature of the coaching interaction, the role of media in coaching is certainly more than delivering messages like parcels. Rather than a linear, cause-effect relationship, a communication process like coaching is ever-evolving (Bachkirova, 2016). During the coaching dialogue, coach and client engage in a joint exploration of the client's experienced reality, values, and assumptions. This collaborative exploration and construction of meaning fosters clients' reflection and problem-solving processes and it leads to mutual learning and new insights. The coach and client influence one another, as their verbal and non-verbal acts and their reactions to these acts, their perceived identities, expected behaviour from their conversation partner, as well as the contents of communication all influence the dynamics of the relationship (Scholl, Lackner, & Grieger, 2016). These evolutionary exchanges facilitate coaching clients' problem-solving processes.

Interlocutors play an active and constructive role in the communication process (Kozma, 1991, p. 179). As discussed earlier, the intended message being transmitted may differ from the interpretation of the same message by the receiver, as for instance when the sender insinuates something, uses a metaphor, or is being ironic (Searle, 1975, p. 59). The content of a message and how it is articulated can be influenced by different factors, such as how speakers wish to be perceived, or by their perceived role identities, and the behaviour they expect from their conversation partner (Scholl, Lackner, & Grieger, 2016). Communication messages may also be influenced by other implicit socio-emotional dimensions – agency or passivity, and striving for social connections (see Bakan, 1966). Figure 2.2, illustrates the different factors that influence how communication messages are articulated and expressed and how they are perceived.

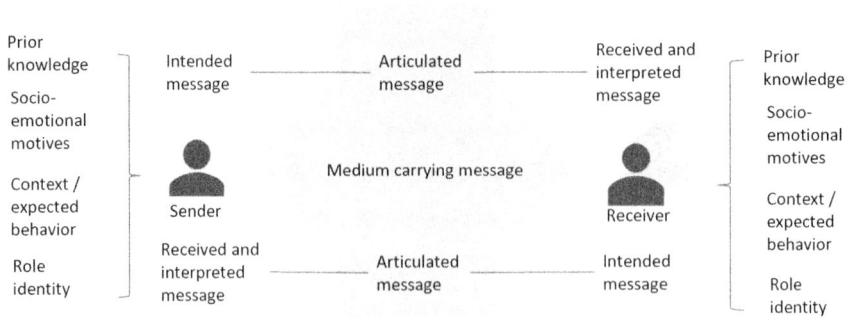

FIGURE 2.2 The constructivist communication model

What do we mean by coaching media?

Media are used to convey implicit and explicit messages that are directed at the client or the coach, typically with the intention to evoke a reaction or response, and they may involve linguistic, non-verbal, and paralinguistic communication (e.g. tone, volume, and pitch of voice, speed of speech, facial expressions, gestures and postures) (Geißler et al., 2014; Luhmann, 1986; Watzlawick, Beavin, & Jackson, 1967).

Coaching media are not used in a free manner, but in a structured one (Geißler et al., 2014). The use of media within a coaching context is different from using interpersonal communication media in a non-professional, informal conversation, in that the coaching communication process is always shaped by coaching methodology.

Drawing upon Searle's (1975) speech act theory, Geißler (2009, 2015) indicated that coaching communication can be broken down into sequential sense units, each of which – aside from the coaching issue that is conveyed through a medium – involves an intention and a methodological structure. The intention – corresponding to Searle's (1975) concept of the illocutionary act – represents the client's desire to solve the coaching problem through the coach's guidance and support. The coaching dialogue is methodologically structured through sequences of speech act, which purport to guide the client in solving the coaching issue (Figure 2.3).

Whilst media enable coach and client to exchange content and to co-construct meaning, it is the methods and techniques (for instance, asking reflective questions, active listening, and mirroring) that guide the structure of these contents. In this sense, media differ from methods (Clark, 1983, 1985; Geißler et al., 2014). At the same time, making a clear distinction between media and methods is rather difficult, as there is an integral relationship between the two (Kozma, 1991). Media may (or may not) incorporate methods. For instance, computer-assisted learning (CAL) is a learning strategy that integrates the use of computers and may involve specific methods, such as simulations and demonstrations. Similarly, a text-based coaching program incorporates a methodological coaching structure. Verbal expression and body language are communication media, whilst not necessarily coaching media.

Coaching medium

Intention ← → Structure

Coaching issue

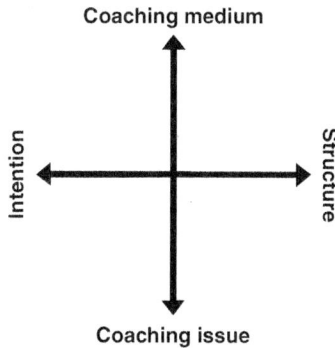

FIGURE 2.3 Aspects of the sense unit in the coaching process (Adapted from Geißler, 2015).

When used within a coaching context, they are structured by coaching methods and specific techniques, such as reflexive coaching questions, role play, or coaching exercises. Similarly, audio and video telephone conferencing are not coaching media per se, but they become coaching media, when they are used by the coach to intentionally guide the client's outcome-oriented reflection. A doll can be used in coaching to help the client visualize a relationship with someone in his/her social circle (Geißler et al., 2014, p. 139). In this sense, the doll – which otherwise would not be a coaching medium – becomes a coaching medium in that it is used along with the coaching method of visualization. Digital tools, such as a simulation tool can be used by a coachee under the guidance of a coach to map out and visualize a problem situation, and to seek ways to position and reposition its parts in a way that could represent a solution to the coachee's problem. Methods can also influence the choice of media. If we use a simulation method, we might choose a computer-based virtual world as the medium. If we use a demonstration, we might choose PowerPoint slides as the medium, rather than plain text.

Using new media to facilitate the coaching dialogue

Face-to-face communication allows us to use multiple human senses to exchange messages. It allows us to use verbal language and auditory cues to receive messages in real-time. It also supports non-verbal cues, including facial expressions, body language such as, posture and hand gestures, the tone of voice and speed of speaking. It allows us to smell, touch, and feel the presence of the other person in the room, and it allows us to communicate while being in the same context.

When coach and client communicate remotely, 'new media', that is computer-based media and telephones are used as the physical carriers of their communication messages. McLuhan (1964) considered media as extensions of our senses. The telephone being the extension of our hearing and voice, enables us to speak to and hear another person from a distance. Text being the extension of our speech, enabling us to communicate our thoughts even if the other person can't see or hear us. Avatars being the extension of our bodies and of our physical presence. Media in this sense, expand the reach of our communication messages. When the exchange of coaching messages is enabled by new media however, sensory information is reduced to fewer senses or even to mono-sensory communication (text) and communication lacks contextual cues to various extents. So, how might these media affect the understanding of clients' intended meaning?

The coaching pair actively engages with the medium and uses it to get their message across and to be understood. Through media, we can see, hear, read, and interpret information. Depending on the nature and qualities of a medium, the communication message could be expressed and perceived differently. For instance, a message that is transmitted through a text medium can have a different meaning when it is written from when it is read (Chandler, 1994). Or text-based media might even encourage different communication content than face-to-face media. In other words, media produce a certain experience, and different media can produce different experiences.

Given the importance of non-verbal cues for decoding communication messages and for understanding clients' (and coaches') intended meaning, one might presume that media that lack sensory cues, prevent us from exchanging non-verbal information and might constrain communication. Many coaches and clients may be suspicious of whether text-based communication has the capability to accommodate rich and meaningful coaching exchanges and to lead to positive results. This view becomes even more pronounced when dealing with sensitive coaching issues. Indeed, the type of coaching issue and coaching context were found to be major factors for media selection in both, Charbonneau's (2002) and Frazee's (2008) studies, which indicated that face-to-face coaching was preferred for emotionally complex issues and for coaching executive clients. These findings support some of the available theoretical literature. Daft and Lengel (1986) proposed and empirically demonstrated (Daft, Lengel, & Trevino, 1987; Daft & Lengel, 1988) that rich media, that is media which allow multiple sensory cues and immediate feedback (e.g. face-to-face communication) are more suitable for resolving uncertainty and ambiguity in conversations than lean media. In a similar vein, the earlier theoretical model by Short, Williams, and Christie (1976) proposed that media affect interpersonal communication based on their levels of social presence, how salient the other person is in the interaction (p. 65), which might be achieved through eye contact and physical proximity and through both verbal and non-verbal communication messages. From this perspective, seen along a continuum, face-to-face contact allows a higher degree of social presence and offers a higher level of richness than video communication, followed by audio-based media and subsequently, by online text-based communication. The latter could be considered impersonal and devoid of non-verbal cues.

However, several subsequent studies (a.o. Dennis & Kinney, 1998; Hancock, Thom-Santelli, & Ritchie, 2004; Kinney & Watson, 1992) have disproved these theoretical propositions. Even though face-to-face media allow verbal and non-verbal communication, and thereby more information can be transmitted at a time, it has been indicated that leaner media, such as computer-mediated communication can lead to equally strong relationships as face-to-face communication, even though relationships over computer-based text media may take longer to be established (Walther, 1992, p. 80; Walther & Parks, 2002, p. 535); an observation that has also been supported by several counselling and psychotherapeutic research studies (a.o. Barak et al., 2008; Cook & Doyle, 2002; Murphy, Mitchell, & Hallett, 2011; Rice & Love, 1987).

If both rich and lean media can support interpersonal relationships, it is useful to explore how different media along the richness continuum might shape the coaching experience, depending on their capabilities for instance, to convey emotional and contextual cues, to support focus on the coaching contents, or to enable a flowing conversation. The following sections offer insights into coaches' experiences with different media – video communication media, avatar worlds, audio and text media, and asynchronous modes of communication – based on an empirical study (Kanatouri, 2018), described in the Introduction. The discussion is enriched by providing participants' direct quotes. Insights into coaches' and clients' experiences with different media are also offered by other empirical coaching studies.

Video communication

Video-based communication media, such as video calls (e.g. Skype, Zoom), HD videoconferencing (e.g. GoToMeeting, ClickMeeting), and asynchronous video messages (e.g. via WhatsApp) allow auditory-verbal cues and visual contact to the client. Along with verbal communication, coach and client obtain clues about each other's thoughts and emotions based on their facial expressions and gestures.

Video communication media offer many advantages, but they also have potential weaknesses. The availability of visual cues during video communication on one hand might be helpful for building trust and rapport (Kanatouri, 2018). On the other hand, visual contact might distract from the coaching conversation (Chen, 2002; Garfinkel, 2005; Hancock, 2014; Kanatouri, 2018). Interviews with coaches (Kanatouri, 2018) have revealed that visual contact is not always helpful or desirable. In coaches' own words:

> I think with the camera off I get a different sense, so my attention is taken to the voice and not distracted by the visual.
>
> Visual cues can be very distracting. So, I'm the kind of person that, when looking at someone and they have a hair that's out of place, that will distract me, so it reduces my ability to focus and concentrate as a coach.
>
> *(Source: Kanatouri, 2018)*

Even though video communication allows rich sensory information exchanges, it reduces the experience of the coach and the client to the computer screen and in this sense, it differs significantly from face-to-face communication. Seeing the coach or the client face-to-face is not the same as seeing the coach or the client on a computer screen. The poor picture quality, particularly in the more inexpensive video communication media such as Skype video calls might prevent the subtleties and nuances of clients' facial expressions from coming through (Lapidot-Lefler & Barak, 2012, p. 436; Kanatouri, 2018). As one coach described:

> the detail, the small movements of the facial muscles that can tell us so much are missing, and these are crucial to raising our awareness to the coachee's emotional state.
>
> *(Source: Kanatouri, 2018)*

Deniers (2017) explored the impact of the camera during Skype video calls on clients' experience of being coached, also concluded that copresence in the form of a physical, face-to-face meeting is not the same as telepresence. Despite the fact that visual contact was valued by clients in her study, they also experienced feelings of uncertainty and nervousness when speaking to the camera, and they perceived the coach's presence as being 'reduced' to voice and facial expressions (Deniers, 2017, pp. 22–25). Visual contact is restricted mainly to the coach's or client's head, and provided that the camera is adjusted, the hands. Even though visual contact is available, eye contact in communication via webcam tends to be inaccurate. As the camera is not placed at eye level, communication partners tend to look at the screen, rather than directly at the camera. This technical limitation could create a challenge for assessing clients' emotions.

> Lag is obvious and there, also the eye contact cannot be accurate, as the camera is never at eye level. People look at the screen, not at the camera.
>
> *(Source: Kanatouri, 2018)*

Moreover, video communication may occasionally be disrupted, if the internet connection is weak, and time lag is also rather common, at least with Skype video calls. The client suddenly becomes aware that the coach can be 'turned off' at any time (Deniers, 2017).

Despite these challenges, the use of video calls in coaching has increased over the years (Sherpa, 2012, 2019) and given the continuing advances in technology and faster broadband internet connections, we can expect that the use of video communication in coaching will continue to increase. Already tools such as Zoom offer improved solutions. Picture quality will continue to improve over time, whilst time lag and disruptions may become less common, allowing smoother and more positive coaching experiences.

Audio communication

When using audio-based media (e.g. telephone, VoIP calls, asynchronous audio messages), visual and contextual cues are absent. Despite that, empirical evidence suggests that strong rapport between coach and client can be developed via telephone communication (Ghods, 2009; McLaughlin, 2013), and it can lead to positive and sustainable coaching outcomes (Ghods, 2009, p. 124).

A challenge with audio communication is that the absence of visual cues doesn't allow to match clients' verbal expression with their facial expressions, gestures and body language. In this sense, the lack of visual contact could inhibit the assessment of clients' emotions (Charbonneau, 2002, p. 80) and it could potentially create a challenge for maintaining silent moments during the coaching dialogue for the client to reflect (Clutterbuck & Hussain, 2010, p. 19). As one interviewed coach expressed:

> you don't have any visual cues of the other person and silence is very difficult to maintain, because if there is silence on this side of the line, you think they are dead, or you have been cut off or something. It's much more difficult to use silence, because you can't see the client, therefore it's a lean conversation, what you do is, you fill the spaces. There is a lot more talking going on, and very little reflection.
>
> *(Source: Kanatouri, 2018)*

On the other hand, telephone communication may not entirely prevent non-verbal communication. For instance, focusing on clients' tone of voice or manner of speaking allows experienced coaches to obtain insights into clients' emotions and thoughts (Clutterbuck, 2010, p. 18). Some studies have pointed out that the lack of visual cues could even enhance focus on the content of the coaching conversation (Charbonneau, 2002; Geißler et al., 2014; Kanatouri, 2018; McLaughlin, 2013). The reliance on clients' verbal cues only, means that coaches can tilt their attention solely on clients' words and way of speaking, which allows them to focus strongly on the content of communication, without being distracted from visual inputs:

> you focus on the actual conversation. The looks of the client, or the looks of the coach, the surroundings, everything else, does not play a role at all, you don't perceive it. So, all we've got for our communication process is the topic as such. So, I'm not distracted by the face, I am not distracted by body language, for instance.
>
> *(Source: Kanatouri, 2018)*

The very distance of the client that is in a way, exacerbated by the absence of visual contact, possibly creates at the same time a feeling of emotional safety and intimacy, which supports clients' transparency and self-disclosure (Kanatouri, 2018; McLaughlin, 2013, p. 5). In coaches' own words:

I find phone coaching takes me deeper and often is more intimate in what the client shares, maybe because they feel safer with sharing over the phone as there is some distance.

If you don't see the person face-to-face, it's easier to be completely transparent. You don't have to keep up appearances, you don't have to manage the perspective or the opinion of the coach. So, the relationship that's built between the client and the coach can be far more intimate.

(Source: Kanatouri, 2018)

3D graphical self-representation with audio/text-based communication

Desktop-based, or immersive Virtual Reality applications often accommodate audio and/or text chat to facilitate communication. Other than face-to-face visual contact, avatar-centric interaction allows the coach to see a 3D virtual representation (avatar) of the client (and vice versa). Unlike video communication, where coach and client see each other in a separate context in their screen, the coach and client avatars can be placed next to each other to have a conversation. The virtual environment in which the interaction takes place could create a sense of presence for the clients (Andrews, 2014, pp. 141–142, see Box 2.1), as clients immerse themselves in the environment they are part of, and focus on their behaviours or actions. The coach obtains contextual information, as the client might choose a landscape they wish to be in, such as a beach or a forest, and may select objects and artifacts that have symbolic significance for him or her. These can be used as a basis for the coaching dialogue.

According to interviews with coaches (Kanatouri, 2018), a potential challenge with placing the coaching dialogue in a virtual reality environment, particularly for inexperienced users, is the learning curve involved in learning the controls to manipulate. As one of the coaches explained:

The biggest issue with virtual reality is the time it takes to learn how to use it and navigate – detracting from the coaching engagement (or any learning engagement). Most people find it easier to describe their situation with language than to build a representation of their world.

(Source: Kanatouri, 2018)

BOX 2.1 COACHING IN SECOND LIFE®: A CASE STUDY RESEARCH

A case study research by Andrews (2014) set out to explore the suitability of the virtual world, Second Life® for coaching. Eight coachees received four group coaching sessions in Second Life®, with the aims to improve work performance and personal well-being. Data was collected through direct observations of the process, through participants' reflective journals and semi-structured interviews with each participant after completion of the coaching program. Several participants reported positive perceptions of their coaching experience in Second Life®, as they felt that this virtual world permitted them to have a sense of presence and to immerse themselves in the experience. At the same time, a few of the participants reported negative experiences, but these were attributed by the researcher to their low level of expertise with virtual worlds or to a bad internet connection, which impacted communication with their coach. Overall, as the researcher concluded, Second Life® is a feasible technology for delivering coaching.

Source: Andrews, A. R. (2014). *Avatar coaching: A case study on the perceptions of virtual reality coaching interventions with an avatar coach*. Unpublished doctoral dissertation, Capella University, USA.

As technology advances, as more users are comfortable with using this technology, and as the controls for navigating in virtual worlds become more intuitive and easier to use, which is the case with mobile Virtual Reality technology (e.g. the Oculus Quest), the learning curve could become less of a barrier. Discussions with coaches (Kanatouri, 2018) have shown however, that what remains, is the ethical question that could arise when the client reveals an alternative personality in the virtual world (for instance, a criminal personality) that might not correspond to his or her behaviour in real life. What if the client behaves in an unfair or even unethical or unlawful way in the virtual world? Might the client transfer these unlawful virtual acts into reality? Before using virtual environments to facilitate the coaching dialogue, we need to know more about how acting in such environments could be interpreted and transferred to real life actions. One of the coaches in the online community (Kanatouri, 2018) expressed this concern as follows:

> Virtual criminality: how do you ensure an ethical approach in a virtual reality? Having recently found it great using a virtual reality platform in my coaching supervision, a colleague raised an interesting point on the criminal use (i.e. acts that in the real world would be illegal) of such mediums. Which leads me to consider the process of transferring from virtual reality to real world: when it happens, is it safe, what ethical issues are presented, what boundaries you establish, what effect does this have for your session or relationships?
>
> *(Source: Kanatouri, 2018)*

Coaching provides of course a safe space where clients could reflect on the motives and the emotions that are hidden behind such intended actions and where they might identify positive alternative solutions. However, the coach's role and responsibilities, as well as the scope of coaching needs to be clarified in advance and certain boundaries may need to be established; the coach is not a psychotherapist and shouldn't take this role. Working with coaching clients in virtual environments requires specialized coach training and awareness of potential issues that could arise.

Asynchronous communication

Asynchronous media, whether text-based, audio or video messages, allow space for reflection and to carefully consider one's response. In contrast to the synchronous telephone and video communication the contents of which are ephemeral and could be forgotten until the next session, coaches' experience with asynchronous audio, video, and text messages is that these media allow time for them to capture a thoughtfully crafted account (Kanatouri, 2018). Asynchronous messages can be used as documentation, as they offer the possibility for the coach and for the client to return to the record at a later point in the coaching process:

> the mentee or the coachee would send me a note via email to begin with, I'll think about that … I would take time to think about my responses and the answers, and the questions I ask them. They then have time to think about their responses back to me, so if I feel that the quality of the discussion is something that needs lots of deep reflection, so I am positive towards email, because it supports a personal reflection much more deeply.
>
> What you do get online – that you don't necessarily get face-to-face or by telephone – is more opportunities to think deeply about the question posed by the coach, if you are the coachee, also the process of actually writing and putting some words to your thoughts and seeing them on the screen has been found to be similar to the journaling benefits and the writing benefits generally, and other types of coaching and even therapy.
>
> *(Source: Kanatouri, 2018)*

There are similar findings from studies in psychotherapy. Cook and Doyle (2002) suggested that documentation in online text-based psychotherapy was perceived by online therapy patients (n=15) to be useful for re-reading messages from the online sessions and for enhancing their cognitive processing. Another study (El-Shinnawy & Markus, 1997) used a randomly selected sample of 31 individuals of various ranks from a corporation to examine their media choices and found that participants preferred the use of email over voicemail, because of the capability of email to have multiple addressees, but also because it offered a written record of the communication, which could be retrieved at a later point.

Nowadays however, not only can voicemail and video messages have multiple addressees (for instance, by creating a WhatsApp group and sending the voicemail or video message to all participants), but they can also be easily retrieved at a later point, just like a text message or email can. All three media thus, allow to coach one-on-one (individual coaching), one-to-many (team coaching), as well as many-to-many (peer coaching). Aside from documentation and from enabling communication partners to return to the message, to analyse it and reflect on it, asynchronous media enable coach and client to structure their thoughts, as they can be used to collect and organize ideas. Their usefulness extends beyond the coach–client interaction and problem-solving process, to accompany the client in the transfer of the coaching goal into practice. An example is offered in Box 2.2.

BOX 2.2 USING ASYNCHRONOUS VOICE MESSAGES TO SUPPORT THE TRANSFER INTO PRACTICE

Anna is currently being given more management responsibilities in her work. She is struggling to adapt to this change, as she feels uncomfortable delegating tasks. Her team members sense her lack of confidence. Her coaching goal is to learn how to be more confident as a leader. With her coach, Anna has decided that she wants to try to be clearer and more consequent in her communication with her team. She expects that this will help her show stronger confidence and leadership, and in turn, it will lead to higher acceptance from her team. To achieve this goal, she will prepare her team meetings with her coach and after each meeting, she will evaluate with her coach the team's reactions. Anna has had a team meeting today. Right after, she sends a voice message to her coach, in which she describes how she implemented the action steps she had set out to carry out and how she felt her team reacted. Did everything go according to Anna's plan and expectations of how this would work? This gives the coach the opportunity to follow closely Anna's implementation of action steps and to stay up-to-date with her progress, to encourage and motivate her, or to intervene and help her find an alternative strategy, if the one she currently follows is ineffective.

In addition, video, voice, or text messages can provide useful support to coach training and supervision. Box 2.3 illustrates how asynchronous messaging can be used powerfully as a medium to train practicing coaches and to develop their analytical skills.

BOX 2.3 TRAINING COACHES' SKILLS WITH WHATSAPP AUDIO MESSAGES

The coach training begins by asking one participant to act as the client and the others as coaches. The 'client' sends the group a voicemail, where he describes the coaching issue. The purpose of the first training section is for the participants to practice analysing the coaching issue and gaining clarity over the situation. Each of the 'coaches' replies to the client via voicemail. The 'coaches' have been instructed by the trainer to structure their reply as follows:

Firstly, after listening carefully to the client's voicemail, coaches summarize what they have understood from the client's message. Secondly, they ask one or two questions to prompt the client to offer more information. This might be in response to any unclear, missing, or contradictory information offered by the client. The questions are supposed to help coach and client to gain better clarity of the situation and to define more concretely the scope and the focus of the coaching. The asynchronous medium helps them to learn how to guide the client in this first phase of the coaching process, to analyse the situation and to train in asking questions to obtain a more complete picture of the problem. The medium allows them the opportunity to listen to the client's message several times, time for analysis of the problem and for structuring their response.

Moreover, these asynchronous media enable a higher frequency of the coaching interaction. In between telephone or video-based sessions, the coaching pair can capture and share messages, allowing the coach to stay in touch and to obtain more information about the client, rather than having to wait for the next time that suits both coach and client to have a session. The insights that are captured can be used as a basis for the next coaching session's discussion. An interviewed coach described this advantage as follows:

> So for me, not only do we talk on the phone, but my clients are journaling every day. So, the frequency of contact and the depth of conversation enable us to build rapport very quickly. […] I'm getting more than just auditory cues, I'm getting information or I collect data from their journals. So, the amount of data that I collect overall is vastly higher than I would receive, if I would just meet them once a week or once every two weeks.
>
> *(Source: Kanatouri, 2018)*

The following is an example of asynchronous audio coaching communication via WhatsApp that illustrates how this medium can support the client and the coach in reflecting and structuring their thoughts. As the coach listens to the client, he notices how the client structures his ideas, listens to the client's explicit, but also implicit messages, and pays attention to the client's way of speaking, pauses, breathing patterns and changes in the tone of voice. After having obtained all these clues, the coach complements the client for organizing his thoughts well and for describing the issue in a clear and structured way and prompts the client to consider further and clarify what prevents him from solving the problem.

BOX 2.4 COACHING VIA WHATSAPP AUDIO MESSAGES

Following an initial telephone coaching session, Bill asked his coaching client, John who was struggling with organizing his documents, to describe as clearly as possible the problem he was facing in an audio message. John sent Bill the following message:

'Dear Bill,

As I mentioned in our earlier telephone coaching session, I find it rather difficult to maintain order on my desk. My desk is always full, and my documents are always unsorted. I end up paying fines as payments are over-due and I hadn't noticed them until it was too late. Even though nothing gets lost, I spend a lot of time looking for my documents. I am also uncomfortable when others notice how disorganized I am, and they judge me. Although I know exactly what to do, I just can't seem to manage to overcome this problem.'

Bill listened carefully, not only to the contents of the audio message, but also to the way the client spoke. He noticed that the client spoke about his issue in a clear and calm voice. Bill replied to the client with the following audio message:

'Dear John,

I received your message, thank you for replying so promptly and for describing the issue so clearly and structured. What your message tells me is that you can organize thoughts inside your head very well. I also noticed that you speak very clearly and with confidence. All these are good conditions for solving your coaching issue. I want to summarize what I understood from your message: You said that you have difficulty keeping your things in order. So, you feel that your desk is always full, and your documents are unsorted. As a consequence, you spend a lot of time searching for your documents and you often pay fines for overdue payments. On the other hand, you said that nothing is lost. It is an inner dissatisfaction you have about not organizing your documents and it is unpleasant for you when others see your desk and might judge you. You also said that you know what to do. Nevertheless, you feel that you can't overcome the issue. With that in mind, it seems to me that it's important for you to be able to see more clearly what keeps you from doing what you want to do to keep things organized on your desk. If that's right, this clarification should be our first coaching goal. What do you think about this? It would be nice if you could tell me in a next voice mail. I look forward to your answer.'

Source: Geißler, H. (2018) *Coaching: Methodische Gestaltung elektronischer Coaching-medien*, pp. 28–30.

The capability of asynchronous media to support reflection has been highlighted in several research studies within the coaching arena and online therapy (a.o. Hiltz & Turoff, 1978; Poepsel, 2011; Rochlen, Zack, & Speyer, 2004; Suler, 2004). The enhanced reflection and self-reflection enabled by asynchronous media use has been attributed to the time lag that is inherent in asynchronous media, alleviating the pressure to respond immediately (Suler, 2004). As illustrated in Box 2.4, the asynchronous medium allows time for the client to reflect but also for the coach to carefully analyse the client's message and to provide a thoughtful response. Potential limitations of this type of communication are the rigidity and the lack of flexibility and communication flow, which influence the dynamics of the coaching communication (Kanatouri, 2018). After capturing a message, words can't be taken back and mistakes can't be recovered:

> when committing something to writing – mistakes can be almost impossible to recover from. This means that my contributions when working via online messaging tend to be much more highly crafted – it seems to me that online work trades flexibility in wording for rigor.
>
> *(Source: Kanatouri, 2018)*

This rigidity creates a risk that the intended communication message could be misinterpreted (Byron, 2008, p. 313ff.). Asynchronous text-based media are the leanest media, as communication lacks visual contact, and auditory-verbal and contextual cues, and it doesn't take place real-time. Audio and visual messages allow to reveal undertones and to share emotions more easily in comparison to text. Nevertheless, empirical literature suggests that the absence of auditory-verbal and visual cues in text-based communication media can create a feeling of safety, allowing individuals to articulate their emotions, without feeling embarrassed or fearing that they will be judged (Amichai-Hamburger et al., 2014; Cook & Doyle, 2002). Emotional expression via asynchronous text-based communication media has been linked to the disinhibition effect that is produced, due to the visual anonymity (Bordia, 1997; Joinson, 2001; Sproull & Kiesler, 1988; Suler, 2004; Tidwell & Walther, 2002) and the reduced power dynamics afforded by these media (Bierema & Merriam, 2002; Kiesler & Sproull, 1992). Discussions with coaches (Kanatouri, 2018) support this insight. As one of them described:

> I believe that a lot of undertone and benchmarking of how a person is feeling can be read from the words they do use, and by being able to refer back to what's been said as it's been recorded is also very useful. Language, whether used in a verbal or written form, can tell us a lot about what they are thinking and feeling. And often what's written maybe a more honest and succinct form of what they are trying to say – I suppose it takes away a form of judgment – and it could be a different sort of

courage to let people see what they write, rather than having to verbalize, because they aren't overloaded by how a person is going to react to what's been said.

(Source: Kanatouri, 2018)

Not only may text-based media have the potential to support the conveyance of emotional content (Cook & Doyle, 2002; Derks, Fischer, & Bos, 2008; Rice & Love, 1987), but evidence suggests that individuals tend to adapt their language to compensate for the lack of non-verbal cues in online text-based communication (Walther, DeAndrea, & Tong, 2010, pp. 380–381), and given sufficient time, they establish equally strong rapport online as in face-to-face communication (Walther, 1992, p. 80).

Selecting media for coaching

To varying extents, all media discussed earlier rely on reduced sensory data exchanges as compared to face-to-face presence. The reduced sensory cues might limit the coaching conversation, in terms of its flow and dynamics, and potentially, in terms of how emotions are conveyed and perceived. On the other hand, each of these media also brings distinct qualities to the coaching interaction. Depending on the medium, advantages include documentation, time to reflect in asynchronous chat, and enhanced focus on the client's way of speaking, breathing patterns and pauses, when visual contact is absent. Table 2.1 summarizes the advantages and challenges of these media, discussed earlier in this chapter.

TABLE 2.1 Advantages and challenges of media use to facilitate the coaching dialogue

	Advantages	*Challenges*
Video	Visual and contextual information	Technical challenges may disturb communication flow and cause distractions
	Visual contact might support trust and rapport building	Subtle emotional cues may not come through
Avatar worlds	Context and sense of presence	Learning curve
Audio	Focus on content	Emotional assessment
Asynchronous media (text, audio, video)	Space for reflection Documentation	Lack of communication flow Rigidity
Text (synchronous, asynchronous)	Reduced power dynamics and judgement Disinhibition	Lack of communication flow Rigidity

Selecting a medium to facilitate coaching is subjective and depends on the coach's and the client's preferences and needs. Media Richness Theory proposed that rich media are more suitable for resolving complex issues. However, as several subsequent studies (Dennis & Kinney, 1998; El-Shinnawy & Markus, 1997; Hancock, Thom-Santelli, & Ritchie, 2004; Kinney & Watson, 1992) have suggested, this is not necessarily the case and Media Richness Theory doesn't explain media choices adequately. Several considerations can be made when selecting a medium for the coaching conversation:

Individual sensory preferences

To facilitate a positive coaching experience, it may be important for the coach to consider clients' sensory preferences when making media choices, as these could impact their openness inthe virtual space and the way in which they interact with their coach, what they share, and how they process information and ideas. Some clients wish to have visual contact to their coach and speak to him or her in real-time, whilst others prefer to focus on listening without visual contact, or they may prefer to reflect and respond to the coach in their own time via text. The visual type might prefer video conferencing to the phone, which allows the exchange of verbal and non-verbal cues. The auditory type may be more comfortable communicating via telephone, and the client with kinaesthetic/tactile/interactive preferences might appreciate an interactive virtual environment, a whiteboard tool to sketch out ideas, and text-based exercises (These additional media are described in Chapter 3).

Individual sensory preferences may be influenced by personality dispositions. A study by Hertel et al. (2008) questioned 228 participants with varying levels of extraversion and neuroticism to examine their media preferences and found significant correlations between personality traits and media preferences. Participants high on the extraversion and low on neuroticism scales showed a stronger preference for richer media than introverts and participants high on neuroticism. According to the authors, lean media offered these participants control, and their asynchronous nature protected them from the immediate emotional reactions of their counterparts. So, whilst an extroverted coaching client might prefer video calls, an introverted client might be more comfortable with asynchronous text-based communication and using a reflective journal or text-based questions.

Whilst sensory preferences and personality types could guide decisions when selecting a medium to facilitate the coaching conversation and whilst the primary preference of the client (or team) needs to be considered and respected, it doesn't mean that the possibility of selecting a mix of media should be excluded. For example, video communication between an extroverted client and his or her coach, doesn't mean that the same client can't also write journal entries to reflect in between coaching sessions. Or that a coach should avoid presenting images or other visual tools to a client who prefers text-based communication. A mix of media can be refreshing, enriching and energizing for the coaching interaction, and it can be useful to cover clients' needs in team coaching. In any case, the primary preference of the client needs to be considered and respected.

The medium's usability and performance

The usability and performance of the technology can be an important factor of media selection for seamless implementation in the coaching process. An easy to use, engaging platform and intuitive interface can motivate the coach and client to select a medium, whilst a software that 'crashes' often, a low picture quality or a non-intuitive interface can be frustrating for the coaching pair.

The client's affinity to technology

A very important factor that may influence media selection is the client's affinity to technology. Rather than being an obstacle, technology should enable the coach and client to build rapport and to communicate effectively. It is thus, useful for the coach to assess how familiar clients are with technology, to ask about their user experience and perceived ease of use of these technologies, and to provide support to clients who may be having technical difficulties. Clients who are less familiar and less open to using technology might not respond well if they have to use media that are more complex to learn. Dealing with software that are difficult to navigate and to remember the steps to take, can be overwhelming and discouraging for the client.

The coach-client-medium fit

Not only clients, but also coaches need to be comfortable with the media they use and competent at using them. Moreover, there needs to be a good match between the coach and the client. A research study by Charbonneau (2002), which examined coaches' and clients' media preferences observed that their positive coaching experiences depend on the coach-client-medium fit (p. 122). In other words, there has to be a good fit, not only between the client and the selected medium, but also between the coach and the selected medium, and a good fit between the coach and the client as people.

Alternating between media or combining media

Coaches may choose to alternate between different media, for instance text and video, to take advantage of the different qualities each of them brings. Some media can also be combined, as for instance audio communication during which a visual tool, such as a whiteboard is used to represent ideas. In this way, digital coaching brings together media capabilities to allow enriched exchanges. Box 2.5 illustrates with a fictive example how different digital media can be combined and alternated as necessary in the coaching process.

BOX 2.5 THE COACH'S TOOLBOX TO FACILITATE THE COACHING PROCESS

Anna and her coach, Bill live in different parts of the world. Whilst face-to -face meetings are not an option, digital media can facilitate their coaching interaction. The coaching pair agrees to begin the coaching program with a *video conferencing* session. By using video for the initial session, the coach builds rapport and a personal connection with the client.

Problem clarification and goal setting

In the session that follows, Anna describes the coaching issue to the coach via *telephone*, and the two decide on the scope of the coaching. The coach sends Anna a coaching exercise via *email*, with the purpose to gain more clarity on the coaching issue and situation, as perceived by Anna. The coaching pair discusses Anna's written exercise in the next *telephone* coaching session. This helps Anna to concretize her coaching goal. The coach has summarized in written Anna's situation, as she described it and her coaching goal, and sends it back to Anna via *email*.

Resource activation and action planning

The following *telephone conferencing* session is used for Anna and her coach to explore the positive resources and potential barriers that could prevent her from achieving her goal. For this exercise, they go through a selection of *symbolic images*, which the coach shows Anna using *screensharing*. Anna and her coach discuss these images and her associations of them to her situation. In a subsequent session, coach and client brainstorm different alternatives for Anna to accomplish her goal. During a video conferencing session, they use a digital *whiteboard* to sketch alternatives and to define concrete actions towards goal attainment.

Support in transfer of actions into practice

Bill asks Anna to send him a *voicemail* after implementing each of these actions, and to describe how successful her attempt was, or if there were any unexpected events that prevented her from carrying out the action. The first attempt didn't go according to Anna's plan. Bill listened carefully to her message and suggested a follow-up *telephone* coaching session where the coaching pair reviewed the action plan, considered the reasons why the action implementation had been unsuccessful and discussed alternative routes and actions. Shortly before implementing her action as intended, Bill sent Anna a *voicemail* to motivate and encourage her. After implementing the desired change and reaching her goal, Anna and her coach meet once again in a *video conferencing* session to evaluate the coaching process.

Ethical considerations

The use of digital media involves ethical risks that should by no means be neglected. Particularly, data breaches are an important concern as they compromise client data privacy. Questions about software encryption and secure record storage are thus, necessary to address when choosing media for the coaching process. Ethical issues that could arise during digital coaching processes are discussed further in Chapter 5.

Other considerations

Other factors that may play a role in media selection are clients' and coaches' expectations and openness to using technology. A research study by Charbonneau (2002) for instance, found that executive coaches felt that they were expected to deliver coaching face-to-face and they believed that their clients wouldn't accept remote coaching for the high rates they were being charged. Surely, a lot has changed since then and as positive empirical evidence supporting the efficacy of technology-mediated coaching accumulates, the assumption that technology cheapens the process appears increasingly outdated. There may still be cases however, where coaches and clients have a negative attitude towards certain media, or they are negative towards technology-mediated communication altogether, or where they don't believe that remote sessions can be effective and that digital media can enhance the coaching process. In these cases, digital media might still be selected, out of necessity (if face-to-face contact is not possible), or as an add-on, in between sessions, or simply for sharing resources or for conveniently carrying out administrative tasks.

Questions for reflection

- What could be the risks involved for the coaching interaction, when the coaching dialogue is reduced to fewer senses? What do these risks depend on? Consider different ways in which these risks might be avoided.

- Can some media constrain rather than support the coaching communication? Does this depend only on the medium? What other factors could play a role?
- Consider the contextual cues available in face-to-face communication. How does contextual information in video communication differ from face-to-face communication?

References

Amichai-Hamburger, Y., Klomek, A. B., Friedman, D., Zuckerman, O., & Shani-Sherman, T. (2014). The future of online therapy. *Computers in Human Behaviour*, 41 288–294.

Andrews, A. R. (2014). *Avatar coaching: A case study on the perceptions of virtual reality coaching interventions with an avatar coach*. Unpublished doctoral dissertation, Capella University, USA.

Austin, J. L. (1962). *How to do things with words: The William James lectures delivered at the Harvard University in 1955*. London: Oxford University Press.

Bachkirova, T. (2016). Developing a knowledge base of coaching: Questions to explore. In T. Bachkirova, G. Spence, & D. Drake (Eds.) *The Sage handbook of coaching* (pp. 23–41). Los Angeles, CA, London, New Delhi, Singapore, Washington, DC and Melbourne: Sage.

Bakan, D. (1966). *The duality of human existence: An essay on psychology and religion*. Chicago, IL: Rand McNally.

Barak, A., Hen, L., Boniel-Nissim, M., & Shapira, N. (2008). A comprehensive review and a meta-analysis of the effectiveness of internet-based psychotherapeutic interventions. *Journal of Technology in Human Services*, 26 (2–4), 109–160.

Bierema, L. L. & Merriam, S. B. (2002). E-mentoring: Using computer-mediated communication to enhance the mentoring process. *Innovative Higher Education*, 26 (3), 211.

Bordia, P. (1997). Face-to-face versus computer-mediated communication: A synthesis of the experimental literature. *The Journal of Business Communication*, 34 (1), 99–120.

Byron, K. (2008). Carrying too heavy a load? The communication and miscommunication of emotion by email. *Academy of Management Review*, 33 (2), 309–327.

Chandler, D. (1994). *The transmission model of communication*. Retrieved from: http://visual-memory.co.uk/daniel/Documents/short/trans.html.

Charbonneau, M. A. (2002). *Participant self-perception about the cause of behavior change from a program of executive coaching*. Unpublished doctoral dissertation, Alliant International University, Los Angeles, CA.

Chen, M. (2002). Leveraging the asymmetric sensitivity of eye contact for videoconferencing. *Proceedings of the SIGCHI Conference on Human Factors in Computing Systems, April 2002*, 49–56.

Clark, R. E. (1983). Reconsidering research on learning from media. *Review of Educational Research*, 53 (4), 445–459.

Clark, R. E. (1985). Confounding in educational computing research. *Journal of Educational Computing Research*, 1 (2), 137–148.

Clark, R. E. (1994). Media will never influence learning. *Educational Technology Research and Development*, 42 (2), 21–29.

Clutterbuck, D. (2010). Welcome to the world of virtual coaching and mentoring. In D. Clutterbuck & Z. Hussain (Eds.) *Virtual coach, virtual mentor* (pp. 3–30). Charlotte, NC: Information Age Publishing.

Clutterbuck, D., Gannon, J., Hayes, S., Iordanou, I., Lowe, K., & MacKie, D. (Eds.) (2019). *The practitioner's handbook of team coaching*. London and New York: Routledge.

Clutterbuck, D. & Hussain, Z. (Eds.) (2010). *Virtual coach, virtual mentor*. Charlotte, NC: Information Age Publishing.

Cook, J. & Doyle, D. (2002). Working alliance in online therapy as compared to face-to-face therapy: Preliminary results. *CyberPsychology and Behavior*, 5 (2), 95–105.

Daft, R. L. & Lengel, R. H. (1986). Organizational information requirements, media richness and structural design. *Management Science*, 32 554–571.

Daft, R. L. & Lengel, R. H. (1988). The selection of communication media as an executive skill. *The Academy of Management Executive*, 2 (3), 225–232.

Daft, R. L., Lengel, R. H., & Trevino, L. K. (1987). Message equivocality, media selection, and manager performance: Implications for information systems. *MIS Quarterly*, 11 (3), 355–366.

Deniers, C. (2017). *'This is the virtual world and you can only see via this camera' – Experiences of receiving career coaching via Skype: An interpretative phenomenological analysis*. Master's thesis, Birkbeck College, University of London.

Dennis, A. R. & Kinney, S. T. (1998). Testing media richness theory in the new media: The effects of cues, feedback, and task equivocality. *Information Systems Research*, 9 256–274.

Derks, D., Fischer, A. H., & Bos, A. E. R. (2008). The role of emotion in computer-mediated communication: A review. *Computers in Human Behaviour*, 24 (3), 766–785.

El-Shinnawy, M. & Markus, M. L. (1997). The poverty of media richness theory: explaining people's choice of electronic mail vs. voice mail. *International Journal of Human-Computer Studies*, 46 443–467.

Frazee, R. V. (2008). *E-coaching in organizations: A study of features, practices, and determinants of use*. Unpublished doctoral dissertation, San Diego University, USA.

Garfinkel, S. (2005). *VoIP and Skype security*. Retrieved from: www.cs.columbia.edu/~salman/skype/SkypeSecurity_1_5_garfinkel.pdf.

Geißler, H. (2009). Die Inhaltsanalytische "Vermessung" von Coachingprozessen. In B. R. Birgmeier (Ed.) *Coachingwissen: Denn Sie wissen nicht, was sie tun?* (pp. 93–125). Wiesbaden: Springer.

Geißler, H. (2015). *Coaching through modern media, lesson 3, introduction (3): What are media in coaching: A first approach*. Video podcast. Retrieved from: www.e-coaching-education.com.

Geißler, H. (2018). *Coaching: Methodische Gestaltung elektronischer Coachingmedien*. Hamburg: Studienbrief für die Hamburger Fernhochschule (HFH).

Geißler, H., Hasenbein, M., Kanatouri, S., & Wegener, R. (2014). E-coaching: Conceptual and empirical findings of a virtual coaching programme. *International Journal of Evidence Based Coaching and Mentoring*, 12 (2), 165–187.

Ghods, N. (2009). *Distance coaching: The relationship between coach-client relationship, client satisfaction, and coaching outcomes*. Unpublished doctoral dissertation, San Diego University, USA.

Hancock, B. (2014). *The design of a framework and instrument for assessment of virtual coaching competence: An exploratory study*. Master's thesis, Stellenbosch University, South Africa.

Hancock, J. T., Thom-Santelli, J., & Ritchie, T. (2004). Deception and design: The impact of communication technologies on lying behavior. In E. Dykstra-Erickson &

M. Tscheligi (Eds.) *Proceedings of the ACM Conference on Human Factors in Computing Systems*, 6, 130–136. New York: ACM.

Hertel, G., Schroer, J., Batinic, B., & Naumann, S. (2008). Do shy people prefer to send e-mail? Personality effects on communication media preferences in threatening and non-threatening situations. *Social Psychology*, 39 (4), 231–243.

Hiltz, S. R. & Turoff, M. (1978). *The network nation: Human communication via computer.* Reading, MA: Addison-Wesley.

Joinson, A. N. (2001). Self-disclosure in computer-mediated communication: The role of self-awareness and visual anonymity. *European Journal of Social Psychology*, 31 (2), 177–192.

Kanatouri, S. (2018). *Mapping the technology-assisted coaching field: An exploratory study.* Unpublished dissertation, Helmut-Schmidt University, University of the Federal Armed Forces, Hamburg.

Kiesler, S. and Sproull, L. (1992) Group decision making and communication technology. *Organizational Behavior and Human Decision Processes*, 52, 96–123.

Kinney, S. T. & Watson, R. T. (1992). The effect of medium and task on dyadic communication. *International Conference on Information Systems (ICIS) 1992 Proceedings*, 10. Retrieved 10. 11.16 from: http://aisel.aisnet.org/cgi/viewcontent.cgi?article=1050& context=icis1992.

Kozma, R. B. (1991). Learning with media. *Review of Educational Research*, 61 (2), 179–211.

Lapidot-Lefler, N. & Barak, A. (2012). Effects of anonymity, invisibility, and lack of eye-contact on toxic online disinhibition. *Computers in Human Behavior*, 28 434–443.

Luhmann, N. (1986). The autopoiesis of social systems. In F. Geyer & J. van der Zouwen (Eds.) *Sociocybernetic paradoxes: Observation, control and evolution of self-steering systems.* (pp. 172–192). London, CA and New Delhi: Sage.

McLaughlin, M. (2013). Less is more: The executive coach's experience of working on the telephone. *International Journal of Evidence Based Coaching and Mentoring*, 7 June 2013, 7, 1–13.

McLuhan, M. (1964). *Understanding media: The extensions of man* (1st ed.). New York: McGraw-Hill.

Murphy, L. J., Mitchell, D. L., & Hallett, R. H. (2011). *A comparison of client characteristics in cyber and in-person counselling.* Online resource Retrieved from: http://therapyonline.ca/cybercounselling/_protected/resources/Readings/Client_Characteristics_in_Cyber_an d_In-Person_Counselling.pdf.

Poepsel, M. (2011). *The impact of an online evidence-based coaching program on goal striving, subjective well-being, and level of hope.* Doctoral dissertation, Capella University, USA.

Reddy, M. J. (1979). The conduit metaphor: A case of frame conflict in our language about language. In A. Ortony (Ed.) *Metaphor and thought.* (pp. 164–201). Cambridge: Cambridge University Press.

Rice, R. E. & Love, G. (1987). Electronic emotion: Socioemotional content in a computer-mediated communication network. *Communication Research*, 14 (1), 85–108.

Rochlen, A. B., Zack, J. S., & Speyer, S. (2004). Online therapy: Review of relevant definitions, debates, and current empirical support. *Journal of Clinical Psychology*, 60 (3), 269–283.

Scholl, W., Lackner, K., & Grieger, K. (2016). Kommunikation als Methode und als Thema in Coaching. In S. Greif, H. Möller, & W. Scholl (Eds.) *Handbuch Schlüsselkonzepte im Coaching* (pp. 1–11). Berlin and Heidelberg: Springer.

Searle, J. R. (1975). Indirect speech acts. In P. Cole & J. L. Morgan (Eds.) *Syntax and semantics, 3: Speech acts* (pp. 59–82). New York: Academic Press.

Searle, J. R. (1991). What is a speech act. In S. Davis (Ed.) *Pragmatics: A reader* (pp. 254–264). Oxford: Oxford University Press.

Seidl, D. (2004). *Luhmann's theory of autopoietic social systems.* Munich Business Research, Munich School of Management. Retrieved from: www.zfog.bwl.uni-muenchen.de/files/mitarbeiter/paper2004_2.pdf.

Shannon, C. E. & Weaver, W. (Eds.) (1963). *The mathematical theory of communication.* Urbana: The University of Illinois Press.

Sherpa Executive Coaching Survey. (2012). *Seventh annual report.* Retrieved from: www.associationforcoaching.com/media/uploads/publications/Survey-Executive-Coaching-2012.pdf.

Sherpa Executive Coaching Survey. (2019). *Fourteenth annual Sherpa executive coaching survey report.* Retrieved from: www.sherpacoaching.com/pdf_files/2019_Executive_Coaching_Survey_Summary_Report.pdf.

Short, J., Williams, E., & Christie, B. (Eds.) (1976). *The social psychology of telecommunications.* London: Wiley.

Sproull, L. & Kiesler, S. (1988). Reducing social context cues: Electronic mail in organizational communication. *Management Science*, 32 (11), 1492–1512.

Suler, J. (2004). The online disinhibition effect. *Cyber Psychology & Behavior*, 7 (3), 321–326.

Tidwell, L. & Walther, J. (2002). Computer-mediated communication effects on disclosure, impressions, and interpersonal evaluations: Getting to know one another a bit at a time. *Human Communication Research*, 28 317–348.

Walther, J. B. (1992). Interpersonal effects in computer-mediated interaction: A relational perspective. *Communication Research*, 19 (1), 52–90.

Walther, J. B., DeAndrea, D. C., & Tong, S. T. (2010). Computer-mediated communication versus vocal communication in the attenuation of pre-interaction impressions. *Media Psychology*, 13 364–386.

Walther, J. B. & Parks, M. R. (2002). Cues filtered out, cues filtered in. In M. L. Knapp & J. A. Daly (Eds.) *Handbook of interpersonal communication* (pp. 529–563). Thousand Oaks, CA: Sage.

Watzlawick, P., Beavin, J. H., & Jackson, D. D. (Eds.) (1967). *Pragmatics of human communication: A study of interactional patterns, pathologies, and paradoxes.* New York: Norton & Company.

3

DIGITAL SUPPORTING TOOLS

Beyond the coaching dialogue: the role of digital tools in enriching the process

In the previous chapter, we explored how different communication media are used to facilitate the coaching dialogue. Looking beyond the coach–client conversation, additional supporting media can be used to complement and to enrich the coaching process. The use of supporting media, such as drawings or diagrams, clay, materials for creating a collage, and building blocks is not uncommon in traditional face-to-face coaching settings (Schreyögg, 1995, 2012). Such material media offer coaching clients the opportunity to express themselves in various ways, to reflect on their goals, to analyse their problem, to understand what they need to change, and what actions they need to take to solve their problem and achieve their goals (Schreyögg, 1995 as cited in Geißler et al., 2014). Traditional coaching media also appear in the form of immaterial media, which refer mainly to the medium of face-to-face verbal communication between the coaching pair, but also to role play, 'fantasy journeys', and standardized storytelling (Schreyögg, 1995 as cited in Geißler et al., 2014).

Aside from the traditional, physical tools that are used to enrich face-to-face coaching conversations, technology offers the means to enrich the coaching process with a wide variety of digital tools. Telephone, asynchronous audio messages, video calls, asynchronous audio/video messages, synchronous and asynchronous text, and avatar worlds offer ways to virtualize immaterial media and they are essential for the coach and client to communicate at a distance. Beyond these, digital supporting tools also virtualize material coaching media. They are typically used as add-ons to support parts of, or the entire coaching process. Depending on their nature and features, the role of supporting digital tools in coaching may be to:

- Follow up on clients' progress.
- Encourage reflection in between coaching sessions.
- Add structure to the coaching conversation.
- Support perspective taking.
- Offer complementary ways of expression to clients' verbal expression.
- Visualize and analyse the coaching problem.
- Visualize and test potential solutions.
- Automate specific aspects of the coaching process and save time (e.g. strengths assessments).
- Enable client data management (including scheduling sessions and billing).
- Enable marketing and matching.

The effects that digital supporting tools might have for coaching outcomes haven't been researched much at all. Yet, some first empirical evidence provided by Geißler et al. (2014) and Hancock (2014) pointed out the potential of supporting tools to offer value to the coaching process. Geißler et al. (2014) examined 14 coaching clients' perceptions of coaching via telephone and combined with a digital supporting tool. The tool contained predefined coaching questions in text form to accompany coachees in attaining their set goal. Coachees expressed their satisfaction with the coaching they received, and they felt that the supporting tool was helpful in that it added structure to the process. Hancock (2014) explored coaching delivered via Skype video calls combined with another text-based tool with predefined questions. Both coaches and clients who were involved in the study perceived the structured nature of the text-based tool to have a positive impact on the process and they felt that having to type in answers to the questions enhanced reflection and provided a useful documentation. A more recent survey by Huss and Eichenberg (2018) found that new coaching tools, particularly simulations are likely to become increasingly important for visually supporting coaching processes and representing clients' verbal accounts.

Given the rising number of tools in the coaching market, the scarcity of available research to help us understand how might different digital supporting tools benefit coaching clients is surprising. Technology is of course, a moving target and new digital tools for coaching are continuously entering the market. Staying up to date with the state-of-the-art technologies that can be used to support coaching processes and maintaining an overview of how different digital tools can be effectively leveraged to enrich the coaching process could be helpful for coaching practitioners and supervisors, as well as for buyers of coaching services. The different types of tools available and how they can be used to support the coaching process are discussed in the following sections. A distinction is made between coaching-specific tools that have been designed for coaching purposes and in many cases integrate coaching contents, and generic tools, which can be used within the coaching context, but also in other contexts.

Using generic tools in coaching

Generic digital tools are software applications that are available for diverse uses and not only for coaching. Different generic digital tools can be incorporated in the coaching process, such as whiteboard tools, mind mapping software, authoring tools to take notes, to keep a journal or to visually represent ideas, and relevant online resources. The available tools differ in terms of their level of richness, with tools supporting asynchronous or synchronous text, audio, visual, or audio-visual information. Some of them are *interactive* tools and other are *non-interactive* resources. Whilst an article, an audio-podcast or a video are non-interactive tools, the content of which is passively received by the client, virtual worlds, digital Post-it notes and whiteboards are interactive, as the client takes some action: drawing, writing, and acting as an avatar in a virtual environment. Some are *content-free* applications that offer the possibility to create content, and other tools offer *pre-structured* content. Table 3.1 provides examples of different generic tools used in coaching and presents some of their different features.

TABLE 3.1 Overview of generic tool options to support coaching

Types of features	Tool elements	Tool examples
Sensory content forms	Text	Blogs, articles, MS Word documents
	Visual	Online images, whiteboard tools, PowerPoint slides, digital Post-it notes
	Audio/video resources	Podcasts, YouTube videos
Content structure	Pre-structured content	TED Talks, articles
	Authoring tool (content-free)	Word documents, PowerPoint slides, whiteboard tools
Interactivity	Interactive	Virtual worlds
	Non-interactive	Podcasts
Temporal use	Synchronous	Whiteboard tools, used real time via screensharing
	Asynchronous	Video resources watched in between sessions

Generic tools offer opportunities for clients to represent their thoughts and ideas, visually or in written, or to provide relevant contents to the clients' coaching issue that can be used to inspire or motivate them and to drive their reflection processes further. The following are some concrete examples of how generic tools can be used in coaching.

Online resources for inspiration and reflection

Various online resources that address topics, such as, time management, work-life balance, mindfulness, motivating others, reaching goals, succeeding in life, are available on the internet. Relevant online resources might offer new insights or perspectives, inspiration, ideas, and encouragement to the coaching client. Even though their contents may resonate with a coaching client, if they relate to the client's coaching issue, they are considered generic, as they were not specifically created for coaching, but they can also be of interest to wider audiences and they can be used for diverse purposes. Such online resources are publicly available and accessible to anyone. Coaches may locate resources that could be helpful for their clients and share them with them via email or by pointing clients to access them on the internet. Clients reflect on these relevant contents in between coaching sessions and discuss them with their coach during the next session. Online resources are available in the form of:

- Text (e.g. online articles).
- Audio (e.g. podcasts).
- Videos (e.g. YouTube videos, TED Talks).
- Visual content (e.g. a selection of online images, PowerPoint presentations).

Box 3.1 shows a case example of using relevant video resources to the client's issue within a coaching process.

BOX 3.1 CASE EXAMPLE: LISTENING TO AN INSPIRATIONAL TED TALK IN BETWEEN COACHING SESSIONS

Steve is working with a client who wishes to improve her self-confidence. Coach and client delve into the belief structures driving the client's current lack of confidence and they explore how it might show up in the workplace. Steve shares an inspiring TED Talk by Amy Cuddy (2012) on presence and how changing one's body language might make a person appear more powerful and confident. In the coaching session that follows, in addition to internal work on building self-confidence, Steve and his client discuss what they learned from the TED Talk and they agree to attend to and work on the client's non-verbal cues and presence.

Authoring tools to represent ideas and thoughts

To complement clients' verbal expression during the coaching session, authoring tools offer the means for clients to reflect in their own time on questions provided by the coach, in between sessions and to express their thoughts, emotions, and ideas in written. Alternatively, such tools offer clients the opportunity to graphically represent their thoughts in between sessions or during the coaching dialogue. In contrast to the earlier described online resources, the content of which is pre-set and non-interactive or modifiable, the use of authoring tools and interactive visualizations allow the client to create and to modify existing content. The created content can be shared with the coach via email or screen-sharing. Examples of such authoring tools are:

a. *Microsoft Word, Excel spreadsheets, PowerPoint, user-generated video or audio files:* These can be used by clients and coaches to write down their reflections, to illustrate their thoughts and ideas (e.g. using tables and charts), or to create a user-generated video or audio file for the client or for the coach to share their reflections or their observations.
b. *Online whiteboard tools:* They can be used to graphically present information, to sketch, and visually express ideas and thoughts.
c. *Mind-mapping software:* They are used to organize and visualize ideas as part of the one-on-one or the team coaching process.
d. *Other tools for collaborative visualization:* Brainstorming ideas and using Post-its to stick on the visual board (e.g. the Miro tool, see Figure 3.1).

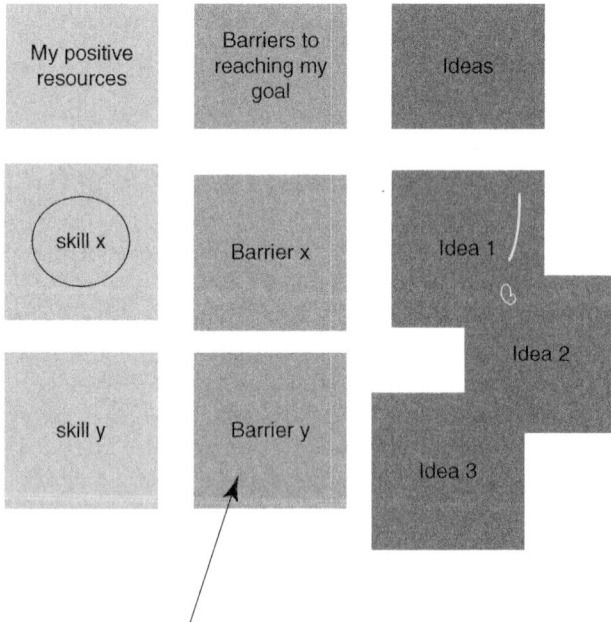

FIGURE 3.1 A coaching session using digital Post-its in Miro

BOX 3.2 CASE EXAMPLE: POWERPOINT SLIDES TO VISU-ALLY REPRESENT AND ANALYSE THE COACHING ISSUE

James wishes to take better care of his own health and fitness levels. Having explained the issue to his coach, James begins to work on analysing the problem in further depth. During a video call, the coach creates a diagram in PowerPoint based on the information obtained from the client, which he shares real-time with the client through screensharing. The purpose of the diagram is to structure all the information already provided by the client, by depicting and better understanding the difference between the actual and desired situation. The diagram (Figure 3.2) divides the actual and the desired situation into four interrelated levels: (1) contextual factors, (2) the client's mental processes, (3) the client's actions, and (4) the consequences of James' actions. The contextual conditions trigger the client's emotions and thoughts about the situation, which become the reason for the client to act. In turn, the client's actions have an impact on the contextual conditions.

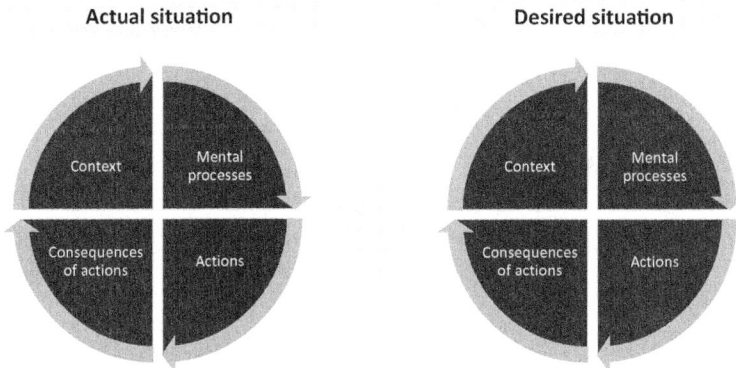

FIGURE 3.2   Actual and desired situation (diagram adapted from the original)

As the coach doesn't have sufficient information to create a complete overall picture of the client's problem yet, he goes on to ask the client the following two questions:

a) *'How does the low priority given to setting time for doing sport relate to the lack of discipline you mentioned?'*, and
b) *'How will you feel when you start seeing first positive effects of your changed behaviour (i.e. doing more fitness)?'.*

Figure 3.3 includes the client's answers. Before continuing with the process, the coach seeks to understand to what extent the client sees the problem as analysed and represented by the coach.

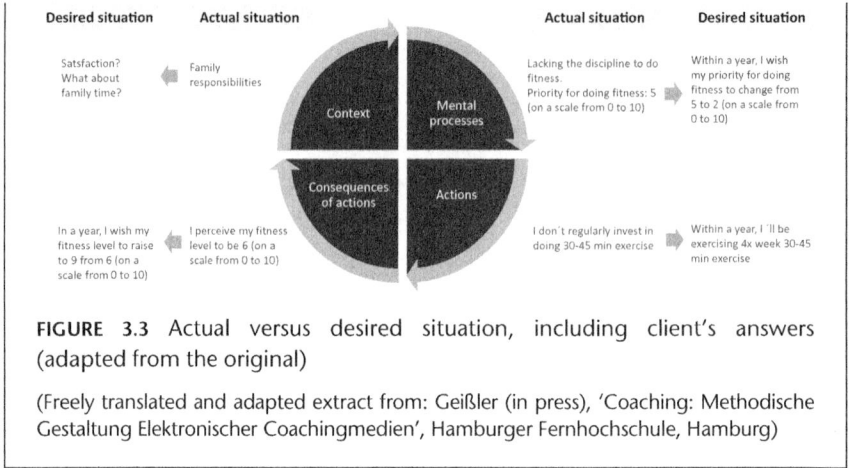

Desired situation	Actual situation		Actual situation	Desired situation

Satsfaction? What about family time? ← Family responsibilities

Context | Mental processes

Lacking the discipline to do fitness. Priority for doing fitness: 5 (on a scale from 0 to 10) → Within a year, I wish my priority for doing fitness to change from 5 to 2 (on a scale from 0 to 10)

Consequences of actions | Actions

In a year, I wish my fitness level to raise to 9 from 6 (on a scale from 0 to 10) ← I perceive my fitness level to be 6 (on a scale from 0 to 10)

I don't regularly invest in doing 30-45 min exercise → Within a year, I´ll be exercising 4x week 30-45 min exercise

FIGURE 3.3 Actual versus desired situation, including client's answers (adapted from the original)

(Freely translated and adapted extract from: Geißler (in press), 'Coaching: Methodische Gestaltung Elektronischer Coachingmedien', Hamburger Fernhochschule, Hamburg)

Exploring perspectives and actions in virtual environments

Online simulation tools such as virtual worlds and scenarios offer the opportunity to explore different perspectives, to test actions and their consequences. Avatar worlds can be used as a standalone medium to facilitate the coaching dialogue, as they typically allow audio and/or text chat. As discussed in Chapter 2, coach and client meet and interact with one another in these virtual worlds. Aside from the coaching dialogue however, such virtual environments provide an additional capability that allows clients to use visual metaphors to express their thoughts and emotions and to explore perspectives, options, and actions. Virtual environments provide context, which could create a sense of presence, engagement of the client in the scenario, and situated learning. Clients, graphically represented through an avatar enter and explore the virtual world by walking, running, flying, or teleporting. They can manipulate objects, simulate real-life situations, and engage in role play. They can act, test the consequences of new behaviours and practice their learned behaviours in a safe environment. Box 3.3 is an example of using metaphor in the virtual world Second Life for different stages of coachees' development.

BOX 3.3 CASE EXAMPLE: 'COACHING IN SECOND LIFE' STUDY BY THE CCL

In 2009, the Center for Creative Learning (CCL) participated with George Mason University and the U.S Air Force to research the feasibility of using the Second Life platform for coaching. The study was funded in part by a grant from the Society for Human Resource Management. Eighteen certified Centers for Creative Leadership coaches conducted fifty feedback sessions in Second Life, recruiting participants from CCL's Leadership Development Program (LDP)®

(Torres, Brodnick, & Powel, 2009). The feedback sessions were designed as two to three hours sessions that allowed the coach and coachee to teleport and meet at the CCL Research Island and Welcome Center. The next teleport destination took them to the Visual Explorer Exploratorium, where the coaching process commences. The coaching experiences included several sensational and colorful simulations that drew them into the full immersive experience of the virtual environment. The coachee selected a picture from CCL's Visual Explore to represent his or her perception of the coaching session and expected outcomes. The coach and coachee teleported to the Assessment Center where the coachee participated in the virtual assessment. Finally, the coach teleported the coachee back to the Path of Understanding, which allowed the coachee to begin the process of development. The Path of Understanding used several virtual landscapes that represent metaphors for different stages of development. The culmination of the journey ended with the coachee looking back at his or her accomplishments from a mountain top and over to the CCL Research Island where the coaching journey began. The integration of virtual world environment with the practice of coaching has demonstrated that there is a usefulness for the platform, for it allows for improved participation and minimal physical restraints; it also offers security and a place for knowledge management and more notably it is fun for the participants.

Source: A. R. Andrews (2014, p. 59)

Purpose-built tools

Unlike generic tools, *purpose-built tools* are designed specifically to support the coaching process. A wide spectrum of coaching-specific tools is available in the market and it includes among other, online question frameworks, assessments, reflective journals, tools for taking notes and for tracking progress, virtual worlds, and constellation tools. These different types of coaching-specific media can be leveraged to support different tasks and phases of the coaching process. Some of them support one specific aspect or phase of the process, and other tools accompany coaching clients in carrying out several different tasks, or throughout the entire coaching process.

One way in which, the different phases of effective goal-pursuing processes can be described, is through Gollwitzer's (1999) Rubicon model of motivation. The Rubicon model distinguishes between (1) the *motivational phase* that involves clarifying one's needs, motives, and problem, and formulating a goal intention, (2) the *volitional phase*, during which, one formulates an implementation intention, and decides on the specifics around implementing goal-oriented action, (3) the *actional phase*, i.e. acting on a selected goal, and (iv) the *post-actional phase*, which involves evaluating the process after action. Greif (2011) discussed the coaching methods that can be used to support clients during each of these phases. Transferring to digital coaching, there are several examples of how digital coaching tools may be leveraged to support coaching methods during different phases and tasks along the coaching process. These examples are discussed below.

The motivational phase: exploring needs and motives and formulating a goal

In the *motivational phase*, the purpose is to help clients clarify their needs and motives related to the coaching issue and to formulate a goal. Through reflexive questions, coaches facilitate clients' self-reflection and reflection on the problem (Greif, 2016). These reflection processes are important for coaching outcomes. As Greif (2016) demonstrated, problem reflection, self-reflection and formulating a goal are among the success factors of coaching. According to the SMART model, coaching goals should be specific, measurable, achievable, realistic, and time-bound, although in many cases it is also adequate to establish more abstract goals (Grant, 2006). Goal definition, reflection, and resource activation are of course not exclusively carried out during the initial phase of the coaching process, but they are recurrent. Coaches guide their clients' problem reflection and self-reflection throughout the process (Schmidt & Thamm, 2008). In the beginning, as Schein (1999) explains, coach and client may not know exactly where the problem lies. Goals could be vague at the beginning and they might also need to be redefined at a later point.

Beyond the face-to-face or distance coaching dialogue between coach and client(s), the following types of digital tools may be used to support clients in the process of clarifying their problem and formulating goals.

*   *Journals* allow clients to reflect on a coaching question and to answer in their own time in between sessions.
*   *Predefined coaching question sets* can structure the coaching conversation, and they may guide clients' outcome-oriented reflection between sessions.
*   *Visualization tools*, such as images and constellations to visualize and reflect on the current situation during the coaching session or as part of a self-coaching program.
*   *Goal-setting tools* allow to type in a goal following the coaching discussion or as part of a self-coaching process. As goal setting can be a recurrent process, text tools allow clients to document their goals, which they can then return to, edit it, and redefine it.

Online journals

Online journals encourage coaching clients to reflect and to write down their thoughts to a specific prompt given by the coach. They support clients' thinking processes in between coaching sessions and they may be used for different coaching issues to analyse a problem. They allow clients to reflect on their motivation to solve the problem and their emotional states or thoughts that prevent from reaching a solution. The topics and questions around which clients' journal entries are focused on are specified by the coach, during or following a coaching conversation.

Reflective journals have been found to support self-reflection and critical thinking, and to provide a useful written record and rich insights within management learning processes (Gray, 2007). A qualitative study by Henderson, Napan, & Monteiro (2004) examined the application of reflective journals online and found that online journals enhanced students' insight, cognitive awareness and critical thinking.

JournalEngine™ is a software that allows the coach to send journaling prompts to the client. The client makes journal entries in their own time in between coaching sessions, which the coach can then read and respond to with a comment or a further question. The use of journals might enrich the coaching process in various ways. Interviews with coaches (Kanatouri, 2018) showed that they experienced the use of online journals to be useful for:

- Supporting clients' reflection.
- Allowing coaches to guide their clients' reflection on themselves, their emotional states, their personal experiences and beliefs, as well as for post-action reflection.
- Offering contact frequency, as clients bridge the time in between sessions to work on the coaching issue, and thereby saving time.
- Offering the coach insights into clients' thought processes that might have not been expressed during the coaching conversation.
- Structuring the coaching dialogue, as the clients' thought process is analysed further with the coach.
- Offering documentation.

The example in Box 3.4 illustrates how the coach supports the client by offering prompting questions that encourage him to reflect further and to structure his thoughts.

BOX 3.4 CASE EXAMPLE: WRITING REFLECTIONS IN JOURNALENGINE™

Victor is using the JournalEngine™ software to reflect and write down some of his thoughts and ideas. His coach reads his journal entry and prompts Victor to reflect deeper about the meaning and the potential consequences his decisions and action steps could have on his life and business.

VICTOR: I presented in my forum tonight on living an authentic life. I received some good feedback and as a result I will be presenting them with a vision board for our next meeting among going over my personal mission vision values. I also met with a fellow restaurant owner on the block who offered an interesting partnership in a café/bar he is doing on pier 16. A really great opportunity, lucrative and seasonal (eight to nine months out of a year). Especially with the opening of pier 17. I can put my POS system in because there are only six items on the menu and drinks. We are looking over the plans and deciding if it's worthwhile given my other ventures. It popped in my head that I could put all the restaurants under the management of another entity, a hospitality company, and continue to move my POS agenda and take on more restaurants as a business. But I digress.

The coach prompts the client to consider and reply to the following question in the online journal tool:

COACH: What does authentic living look like? How does it affect your day-to-day actions? How does it affect your business strategy?

Predefined coaching question frameworks

Predefined questions can be used during the coaching conversation, to support clients during or in between sessions, or as part of a self-coaching program. This tool serves several purposes, such as to:

- Structure the coaching conversation.
- Guide clients' reflection.
- Support clients' self-directed, problem-solving capabilities.
- Scaffold clients' progress towards their goal, by breaking down the goal to small, manageable steps.
- Offer contact frequency when used in between sessions, and save time during the coaching session.
- Allow documentation.

Many pre-set coaching question frameworks are designed to support clients throughout the entire coaching process, including coaching support to clarify the problem and to set goals. For example, the tool *Virtual Coaching (VC)* supports coaching clients across four phases of the coaching process: (1) clarifying the issue and the goal, (2) understanding the current situation, (3) setting action steps, (4) implementing an action plan and facilitating transfer to practice, and (5) evaluating progress. Box 3.5 shows an extract from a telephone coaching conversation using the pre-set questions of the Virtual Coaching (VC) tool to support a coaching client during the initial, goal clarification phase.

BOX 3.5 CASE EXAMPLE: USING VIRTUAL COACHING (VC) TO CLARIFY THE COACHING ISSUE

After an initial telephone-based session with Mary, the coach suggested to her to consider and fill out a set of questions in the Virtual Coaching (VC) tool in her own time, until their next coaching session, which was scheduled in one week. The questions were designed to help her identify the most important aspects of the coaching issue and to clarify her goals. Mary answered as follows to the questions below (Figure 3.4):

What is it about?

What needs to positively change in my life?

I´d like to have less stress in my life. I often have too much to do and too many appointments. I often feel hectic, responsible for everything, and quite frequently exhausted or overwhelmed. I´d like to have more time for leisure and relaxation, to be more mindful to avoid being so overwhelmed.

To what percentage does this positive change concern my a) job, b) my private life, c) my health?

a) 20%

b) 50%

c) 30%

With regard to the positive change I wish to have, how high – on a scale from 0 to 10 – is my satisfaction in each of the three areas (job, private life, health) (10= absolutely satisfied)

a) 8

b) 2

c) 4

With regard to the positive change I wish to have, how likely is it - on a scale from 0 to 10 – that I become happier in each of the three areas (job, private life, health) (10= extremely likely)

a) 5

b) 10

c) 10

Importance, difficulty, pressure

How important is – on a scale from 0 to 10 - this positive change for me? (10=extremely important)

10

How challenging is – on a scale from 0 to 10 - this positive change for me? (9= extremely difficult, 10= impossible)

8

To what extent do I feel under pressure – on a scale from 0 to 10 – because this positive change hasn´t yet occurred? (10= extreme pressure)

10

To what percentage is this pressure created by others and to what percentage by me?

Me: 75%

Others: 25%

Thoughts about solving the issue

On a scale from 0 to 10 (10= very precisely) how precisely do I know what I can´t bear or I don´t want to do any longer?

7

On a scale from 0 to 10 (10= very precisely) how precisely do I know what needs to change?

Actions about solving the issue

On a scale from 0 to 10 (10= very precisely) how precisely do I know what I need to do for the positive change to happen?

7

On a scale from 0 to 10 (10= extremely important) how important is my personal development to me?

FIGURE 3.4 Virtual Coaching (VC)

Source: Coaching session with Prof. Dr. Harald Geißler

In the next telephone coaching session, Mary and her coach discussed her written answers. The coach noticed that Mary had selected an image to represent her coaching goal:

COACH: What do you see in this picture and why does this picture resonate with you?

MARY: The picture shows rocks and the sea. It represents my need to achieve calmness, clarity, order, and movement. Exactly what I wrote there, namely calm, clarity, order, and movement. I see the peace in the open sky and the sea. I see clarity because there are no clouds in the sky. The rocks symbolize the order and the waves symbolize the movement I wish to have in my life.

COACH: What is the relationship between the four keywords, peace, clarity, order, and movement, to your answer: 'I'd like to have more time for leisure and relaxation, to be more mindful to avoid being so overwhelmed'?

MARY: I am not quite sure, but what is clear is that the picture shows the calmness I want to achieve.

Even though Mary is sure that aside from calmness, the other three words, clarity, order, and movement are also important to her coaching goal, she is unable to articulate her intuition clearly. The coach decides to give her an impulse:

COACH: I have the impression that order is particularly important to your coaching goal. If so, the question arises of what kind of order you want. Is it more that you want to bring more order or a different order into your life? By saying 'a different order' I mean an order so that you can achieve what you want, that is so you have time for leisure and relaxation, that you are mindful and not overwhelmed as you said. How does this idea sound?

MARY: This idea sounds right to me. A different order would mean that I am able to set priorities for things I have to do, whereas at the moment everything is 'priority 1' for me. So, I want more clarity as to what is important and what is less important.

COACH: Great, I think what you just said is very important. Would you like to write it down in the tool so that this idea doesn't get lost?

MARY TYPES: It's important to me to build a different order, in which I have clarity and I can prioritize my actions.

In the last ten minutes of the session, the coach asks Mary to describe as precisely as she can, what kind of support she expects from the coach over the following sessions.

MARY TYPES: I want to understand what I can change personally so that I am less stressed and so that I find peace. I would like my coach to accompany me in my endeavour to implement my goal to be more relaxed in my everyday life. The coach should keep reminding me to stay focused on my goal.

The *CoachMaster*™ software consists of predefined question sets based on the GROW model, for different coaching issues, such as career, health, time management, or team conflict issues. The tool can be used during a telephone coaching session or in between coaching sessions as a standalone, text-based communication medium. The questions take the client from establishing a clear goal, to exploring the current reality, obstacles, and options, through to determining an action plan. The following example in Box 3.6 is an extract from a coaching session, illustrating how the coach uses the pre-set questions in the software to support the client in defining her coaching goal and session goal.

BOX 3.6 CASE EXAMPLE: GOAL SETTING WITH COACHMASTER™

COACH: Hi Jane. What would you like to work on in this session?

JANE: I've been given more responsibilities at work, which requires me to be more of a leader. I'm finding I am having trouble with the mentoring aspect of it.

COACH: Can you say more about what aspect of mentoring causes your problem?

JANE: Well, I'm not comfortable telling people what to do, and I also think people question whether or not I know what I'm talking about.

(The coach uses one of the built-in questions in the software to help Jane become clearer about her overall objective.)

COACH: If you did feel comfortable doing those things what would somebody watching the scene from outside actually be seeing and hearing that would indicate that you have succeeded? Or is it more an internal experience? Internal to you that is!

JANE: I do think a lot of it is in my own head. I suppose if someone were to see successful mentoring in action, they would see someone who is confident, know what they are talking about and person being mentor would be receptive.

COACH: So, the goal is to be confident while mentoring and have the other people be receptive?

JANE: Yes, I suppose it is. I also have this negative internal dialog about all the judgments I think the other person is making. I worry that the person will not like me if I'm 'telling them what to do' or that they do not think I'm smart.

(The next question I tried is one of the standard coaching questions built into CoachMaster™, which is popularly known as 'The miracle question'. It comes from brief therapy.)

COACH: Thanks Jane. If you woke up tomorrow and the problem had magic-
ally disappeared, how would you know?

JANE: I would have a good working relationship with all my colleagues and no
negative thoughts regarding what they think of me.

*(Jane's answer is good in terms of being clear what she would like but unrealis-
tic in terms of normal human relationships. I then try and focus Jane on a goal
that might be more in her control. Because one thing we can't control all the
time is what others think of us.)*

COACH: Could we focus on the negative thoughts about what they might be
thinking about you? How about a goal to give mentoring and not be
overly affected by what they are thinking? You can focus on the other
parts if you wish – the positive working relationships.

*(So, I suggest a goal which should be more in Jane's control. You might see
that it is not completely SMART. This is something we actively encourage on our
training as we have discovered with text coaching it is easier to get distracted
trying to get a perfectly SMART goal when the real value is further on in the
process. But I do give Jane a choice and I ask her for a date to keep focus.)*

JANE: The first goal works for me.

COACH: By what date do you want to achieve your goal(s)?

JANE: By the end of the month

*(Goal Statement updated: 'to give mentoring to my colleagues and not be
overly affected by what they are thinking by the end of the month. Stage
changed to Session Goal in CoachMaster'. We now come to the Session Goal
which is what the client wants to have accomplished by the end of the
session.)*

COACH: What would you like to gain from this session?

JANE: A plan of how to achieve my goal.

Source: Griffiths, R. (2017)

Visual tools

Predetermined text-based questions can be combined with visual tools, to
enhance clients' reflection. For instance, the *Symblify*® self-coaching app supports coachees in clarifying and describing their problem in writing, and it also
allows them to visualize the problem and to explore their motives, needs, and
emotions with the help of symbol cards (see Figures 3.6, 3.7, 3.8).

BOX 3.7 CASE EXAMPLE: VISUALIZING POTENTIAL SOLUTIONS WITH SYMBLIFY®

Amy is an event manager at a company that organizes cultural and artistic events. She is 38 and has two kids. Family is a very important part of her life. She loves her job, but it takes way too much time from her family. Her whole life is a big time-management puzzle, juggling with her colliding roles of being a mother, a wife, and a successful event manager at the same time. Using the Symblify® app, it's easy for her to find the right symbol cards to describe her situation. However, the first surprise is when she realizes that she really loves her job; it's not something she does because of money or responsibility – it's her passion. When she is encouraged to imagine an ideal situation, she suddenly understands that it's not her work but the long business trips that keep her from being with her family. Other activities can be done from home and in a flexible schedule, but travelling is a big, undividable absence from her family. She replaces a few cards and several possible solutions emerge in her mind. She chooses the symbol card showing a puzzle because she finds out that grouping close travel destinations in a more effective way can save her several days in a month. Noticing a card with a little girl on it, she decides to delegate much more responsibility to her younger colleague, gradually training her into conducting negotiations with faraway partners on her own. She also realizes that some of her shorter personal meetings can easily be replaced by Skype conversations. During her 30-minute-long Symblify® session, Amy made a lot of discoveries about her preferences and priorities and decided that she needs to gain more time for her passions: her family and her work.

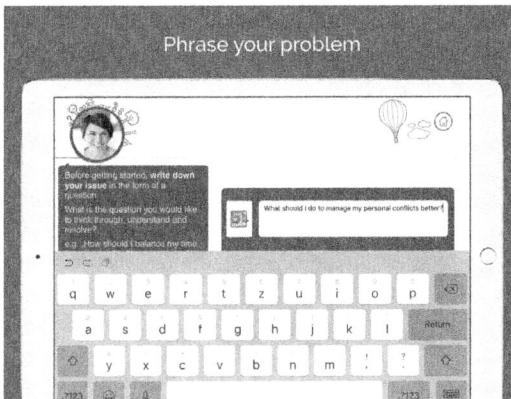

FIGURE 3.5   Symblify® (I)

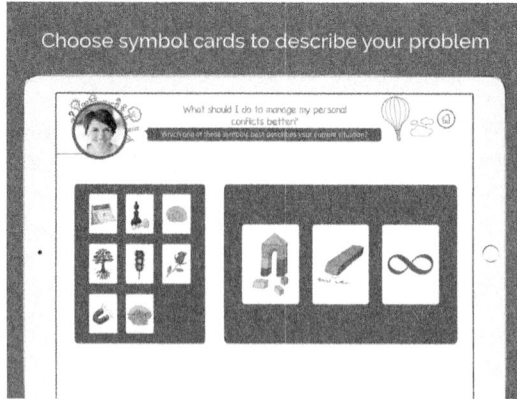

FIGURE 3.6   Symblify® (II)

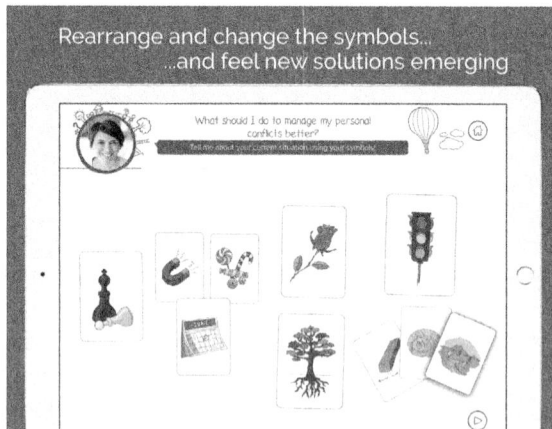

FIGURE 3.7   Symblify® (III)

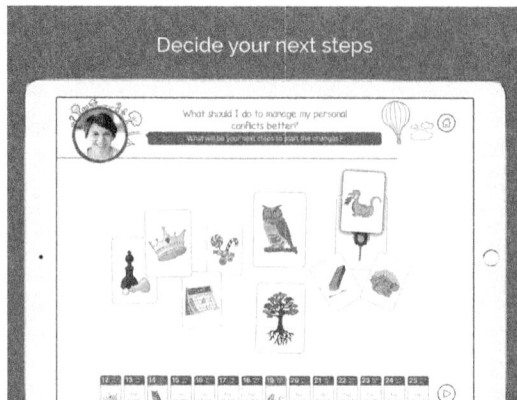

FIGURE 3.8   Symblify® (IV)

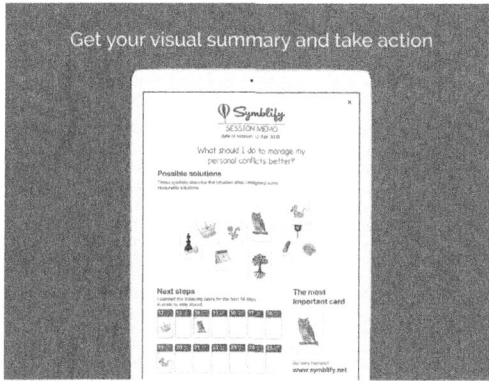

FIGURE 3.9   Symblify® (V)

(c) Copyright 2018–2019 Symagine Lab Ltd., Symblify®

As another example, the text-based tool *Virtual Coaching (VC)* includes a range of symbolic images for the client to select from. In the earlier example of the *Virtual Coaching (VC)* tool (Box 3.5) for instance, the client selected an image showing a beach with rocks. Further images included in the tool are shown in Box 3.8.

BOX 3.8 CASE EXAMPLE: USING SYMBOLIC IMAGES TO SUPPORT CLIENTS' REFLECTION

To support clients' reflection and articulation of the coaching problem, the coach presents a selection of symbolic images and landscapes in the Virtual Coaching (VC) tool and asks the client to look at each of the images and select an image that resonates with her most (Figure 3.10).

FIGURE 3.10   Virtual Coaching (VC) tool

After selecting an image, the coach might ask the client questions such as:

- What do you see in this picture?
- Why does this picture resonate with you?
- Imagine you are in this picture. How does this make you feel? Why?

When reflecting on these questions, clients may gain some clarity about their needs and motives and the situation as it presently is. Guided by the question sequences in the Virtual Coaching (VC) tool, clients type in and save these reflections and new insights, so they can return to them later.

Visual elements can be used to create visual metaphors and simulations for visual exploration and reflection on the client's current and ideal situation from different perspectives. The avatar-based virtual world, *ProReal* is based on Marino's socio-drama and Jung's theory and it is used to enhance telephone coaching sessions, by allowing clients to describe their issue in a visual way. This virtual world includes a landscape with various virtual symbolic elements, such as mountains and hills to symbolize aspirations and goals, a river to symbolize emotions, as well as props, such as a key to symbolize success, a wall and a treasure chest. The tool also provides the opportunity to use avatars as virtual representations of oneself. The avatars are neutrally formed and can be given different postures, colour, size, and captions. The extract below is part of an interview with the developer of the ProReal tool:

> so there is a river running through it, and the river is energy, core energy and quite often people would say emotion. There is a ravine, a place of danger, so when we feel like we are standing on an edge, we go to the edge of a ravine ... there is mountains and hills on the horizon, they are higher aspiration and goals, but we never reach them. There is the woods, the dark woods, we know what it's like to get in the woods, where we can't see out ... there is a castle, there's gateways, so various gateways are transitions from one phase to another ... there is pathways, which are time; normally pathways are the path of time, with crossroads, which are decisions to make; so really each of the features in the landscape are taken from the symbols that are woven into the stories that have been handed down by generation to generation [...]props are all taken from our general use of language, so we might say 'well, the key to success is this', so we have a key we can put in ... or 'there is a wall here between this team and another', so we have walls ... there is a treasure chest ... there is the elephant, we have the saying 'there is an elephant in the room'. So, there are different props that can be used to build texture to the story someone is saying.

(Source: Kanatouri, 2018)

BOX 3.9 CASE EXAMPLE: DESCRIBING THE COACHING PROBLEM IN VISUAL TERMS WITH PROREAL

Clients can select a part of the landscape where they feel comfortable, or which represents their current situation. One client placed himself in the river with his family split on opposing banks. This act alone opened up a useful exploration of the reality of his home situation. Roads can be used as timelines and give the client an axis to move back and forward in time. In a similar way to the use of 'Small World', a client can select avatars to represent people, entities, external stakeholders, or sub-egos. To enable the sociometry to become visible, the avatars can be positioned anywhere in the world and face any direction. In its simplest form, a client will position a number of avatars relative to each other, to represent a family or organizational situation, with the closest relationships next to one another and the most distant individuals further away, thus mapping out a system. The ways in which the world can be viewed are important as they enable perspectives on a paradigm. The design here was informed by Moreno's work and, in particular, the value in seeing the world from another's perspective to build empathy. The platform enables the client to view the world from both first and third person, thus broadening the options for perceiving. In addition, the world can be viewed from a free camera; this means the client can step away from the system and view it from above (or indeed from any angle) to gain a different perspective. The purpose of this is to encourage new thinking, inspired by fresh ways of seeing things. One client has commented on the feeling of being able to 'fly' away from self and view the world from above. The client's world can be shared either in person, or remotely, with a coach. The remote working function enables the coach to work with clients anywhere in the world. A client world in ProReal can be saved and returned to at a later session. It can also be accessed separately by the client, should personal reflection be valued. The User Management system has been designed to ensure appropriate security and confidentiality; for example, the coach creates an individual session which can only be accessed by one client and this process, and access to the system, is password protected. Data protection and security was of critical importance in the architecture of the system. ProReal allows the client to find a voice and to be able to explain her world in visual terms (Figures 3.11, 3.12 and 3.13).

FIGURE 3.11 Using captions in ProReal

FIGURE 3.12 Avatars and symbolic elements

FIGURE 3.13 Using symbolic objects in ProReal software (developers: David Tinker and Andrew Jackson)

Source: Tinker, D. (2013) *'Remote coaching using virtual reality'* Online resource: https://digitalcoach.home.blog/2013/06/09/remote-coaching-using-virtual-reality/ #more-50

On a similar note, *LPScocoon®* is a 3D interactive tool used during telephone (or VoIP) coaching sessions for creating online simulations, developed by Christiane Grabow. It consists of 13 abstract and archaic symbolic forms for the client to place around and to interpret. The coach and client see the same screen and each change is simultaneously seen by both. LPScocoon® allows visualizations of conflict or challenging issues and it helps to clarify complex relationships. Although clients are not restricted in the topics they simulate, the software is mostly used to simulate issues that require a strategic solution, career planning and possibilities, decision-making in business processes, meeting preparation, conflict situations at work, analysis of team and management constellations, and questions concerning the organization. The example in Box 3.10 illustrates how the tool is used to help the client increase awareness of his own perspective and allows the coach to gain a deeper insight into the client's situation as he perceives it.

BOX 3.10 CASE EXAMPLE: SIMULATING SYSTEMIC RELATIONSHIPS IN BUSINESS WITH LPSCOCOON®

Paul is a young project manager who has been recently struggling due to the frequent conflicts among team members to get them to meet the project's deadlines. With the coach's support, Paul specifies his coaching issue: 'How do I get my team to work constructively?' After formulating the question, the coach asked Paul to identify possible factors, such as personal blocks, or values, or anything else that might be preventing him from solving the issue. The coach supports Paul to identify the most essential elements or factors that might contribute in solving the issue. In LPScocoon®, the coach asks Paul to select a form to represent each of the factors or elements that he can use to solve the issue. As the forms are abstract and don't resemble anything familiar, Paul uses his intuition to make associations. As a next step, Paul selects a representative figure of himself and positions his own representative in relation to the other forms, also indicating the direction of their supposed gaze. Deciding on the spatial relationships and on the direction towards which the figures are looking, reveals Paul's personal perspective on the situation. With the support of the coach, thus, Paul observes his inner visualized image, and increases his awareness of the situation from the simulated systemic relationships. The coach enters mentally into the situation of the client and is able to understand his point of view (Figure 3.14).

FIGURE 3.14   LPScocoon® (developer: Christiane Grabow)

Source: Grabow (2013)

Tools to type in and document goals

Numerous digital tools allow clients to type in their goals, either following the coaching discussion or as part of a self-coaching process. By doing so, goals are documented, and clients can then return to them, edit, and redefine their goals at a later point. Examples include the following: *CoachApp24*, *Coachmetrix*, *Coach Simple*, *Goalify*, *Life Coach Hub*, *JournalEngine*™, *Remente*, *Symblify*, and *WorkO-nIt*. For instance, after working with a coach to identify the specific goals they wish to pursue, clients can use the *Coachmetrix* software (Figure 3.15) to document their goals, and then to invite their coach to view their goals, and invite supporters (e.g. team members) to provide them with feedback and encouragement, and track their progress towards these goals over time (see Box 3.11).

BOX 3.11 CASE EXAMPLE: DOCUMENTING GOALS WITH COACHMETRIX

Each goal in Coachmetrix includes a goal title, a behaviour (used to measure Pulse Feedback), and additional goal details. Once the goal has been identified, clients determine a measurable 'behaviour' to associate with the goal. Supporters in the clients' professional environment will be asked to provide feedback. Prompted by Coachmetrix emails, supporters use a brief survey to provide feedback on observed behaviour. The identified behaviour will be an indication of progress toward the accomplishment of the clients' goal.

FIGURE 3.15   Coachmetrix (developer: Sal Silvester)

The difference between the earlier described pre-structured coaching question frameworks and these goal-setting tools is that the latter assume that before clients use these tools to type in their goals, the coaching issue has already been clarified and a goal has been identified with a coach. Unlike the pre-structured questions, which methodically guide clients' problem and self-reflection, goal-setting tools are only used for documenting goals and eventually for sharing them with the coach and other stakeholders.

The volitional phase: formulating a goal implementation intention

Having clarified the coaching problem, and formulated a goal to pursue, during the *volitional phase*, coaches support their clients to formulate a goal implementation intention, to reflect on potential barriers that could prevent them from attaining their goal and to activate and plan their internal and external resources that could help them achieve their coaching goal (Greif, 2011). Self-reflection and reflection on the problem continues through to this phase, following the motivational phase. Resource activation is encouraged, although it may have also started earlier during the motivational phase. Resource activation has been proven to be a success factor in psychotherapy (Gassmann & Grawe, 2006) as well as in coaching (Greif, 2008). Similar to the motivational phase, text-based tools, such as reflective journals and pre-set questions, and tools with pictorial and metaphorical content such as simulations and symbolic images can be used to accompany coaching clients during the volitional phase. Examples of how digital tools can be used to activate positive resources, to reflect on barriers, to formulate a goal implementation intention, and to develop an action plan are illustrated below.

Visual metaphors, simulations, and text-based questions

Coaches can support their clients' resource activation through the use of symbolic images, simulations, and reflective questions. Clients' positive resources can be sought internally, and include personality traits, motivation, competencies and abilities, and externally, including the help and emotional support of family, friends, and colleagues (Greif, 2008).

The *Zurich Resource Model* online tool is a psycho-educative tool that provides resources to optimize individuals' self-management and to support them in the process of pursuing their goals. Using the tool, which is based on the Zurich Resource Model method (Storch, 2004), users are encouraged to spontaneously select images that trigger positive somatic markers – positive feelings and bodily sensations – (see Damasio, 1994) from a selection of images, and then to associate them with words, by selecting from a list of phrases.

The *CAI* institute's web-based platform and mobile apps also offer pictorial contents and text to enable resource activation. For instance, the *CAI® Resource Tree app* (Figure 3.16) allows clients to make annotations on the roots of the resource tree concerning their fundamental values, then on the stems of the tree, about their available strengths, capabilities, and knowledge, and then to the upper crown level, concerning their positive life vision for the future. The app then provides a text field for clients to type in three actions they intend to take to reach their coaching goal.

Reflective journals and pre-structured coaching questions may be used independently or in combination with visual tools to enable clients to reflect on their positive resources, to consider the barriers that might prevent them from attaining their coaching goal, to formulate a clear implementation intention, and to plan their actions. The *Virtual Coaching (VC)* tool provides a structured method of guiding clients through this coaching phase (see Box 3.12).

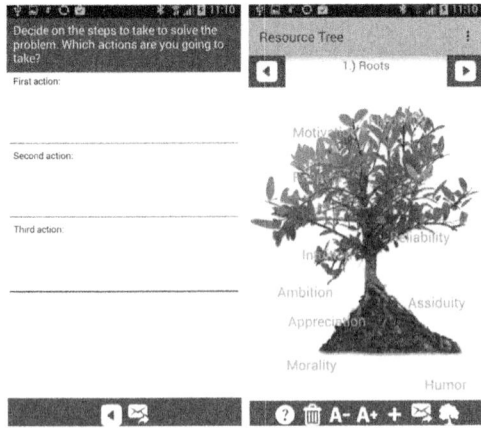

FIGURE 3.16 CAI® Resource Tree app (developer: Dr. Elke Berninger-Schäfer)

BOX 3.12 CASE EXAMPLE: RESOURCE ACTIVATION AND ACTION STEPS DEVELOPMENT WITH THE VIRTUAL COACHING (VC) QUESTIONS

My Coaching goal	My goal-oriented actions until now
What is my coaching goal? What needs to change positively, and by when do I want to have attained my goal?	What is the most important action I have taken to achieve my goal?
On a scale from 0 to 10 (10= extremely important), how important is it to me to reach this goal?	What has the concrete effect of this action been?
On a scale from 0 to 10 (10= extremely challenging, but feasible), how challenging is reaching this goal?	What were the consequences following my action?
My capabilities	**My interim learning goal**
Which are the most important capabilities, motivation and emotions that I curently have, and which I can/want to use to reach my coaching goal? What has prevented me so far from using my capabilities, motivations and emotions to reach my goal?	I imagine that a miracle has happened and the barrier that has prevented me so far from reaching my goal has disappeared, as there has been a positive development in my capabilities, motivation and emotions. What would I do differently to reach my coaching goal from now on? Which capability, emotion or motivation has unfolded in this miracle?
Next goal-oriented action steps	**Further support**
Which concrete steps will I take to reach my coaching goa and my interim learning goal over the next 1, 2 or 3 weeks?	Do I need support for taking the next steps? What kind of support and from who?
To what percentage will I have reached my coaching goal, if I implement these steps perfectly? To what percentage will I have reached my interim learning goal?	When do I wish to check how well I have implemented my planned actions: in 1, 2 or 3 weeks?

FIGURE 3.17 Virtual Coaching (VC) question set

Source: Solution-Finder Module of the Virtual Coaching (VC) tool

Using assessments and surveys to reflect on personal resources

Clients may also explore their positive resources by completing strengths or personality assessments and surveys. Psychometric self-assessments and behavioural feedback instruments, such as 360° feedback can be used prior or during coaching to obtain useful information about the client and to save time. Some coaching-specific software include such instruments. As an example, the software TypeCoach can be used as pre-work to a coaching program. The platform provides interactive videos to explain the different personality types using examples and simple exercises, followed up by an assessment to identify one's own personality type. Alternatively, it is used by teams to see the personality type distribution in their group, with the aim to use their individual strengths and to improve how they communicate and work together. The platform provides interactive videos to explain the different personality types using examples and simple exercises. In addition, it provides tips and techniques that are offered through short texts, videos, and images, to improve one's career potential based on personality type as well to help teams communicate and work effectively together.

Implementation intentions and action planning tools

The *MasterCoach app* owned by 7M Consulting Private Limited in Singapore allows coaches to assign a Strengths Wheel assessment (Figure 3.18) to their client (see Box 3.13). It also includes over 300 coaching questions for the coach to select from, a CoachPad for the coach to take notes and share them with the client, and a Dashboard, where clients update their progress on the agreed action steps.

BOX 3.13 CASE EXAMPLE: THE MASTERCOACH APP

Wan is sales director of a growing business enterprise. This morning, he meets Cheryl, the Product Sales Manager at a nearby café, to coach and review her goals and progress. Wan uses the MasterCoach app to facilitate the performance conversation with Cheryl. Creating 'coaching clients' on MasterCoach is quick and easy. Cheryl gets an email to download the free MasterCoach 'Client App'. Engaging the strengths of others is a powerful way to motivate them. Wan asks Cheryl what it takes to succeed in her current sales role. He uses her ideas to build a 'Strengths Wheel' and sends it to her for a quick strengths' assessment. Cheryl completes and returns the Strengths Wheel to Wan for reference.

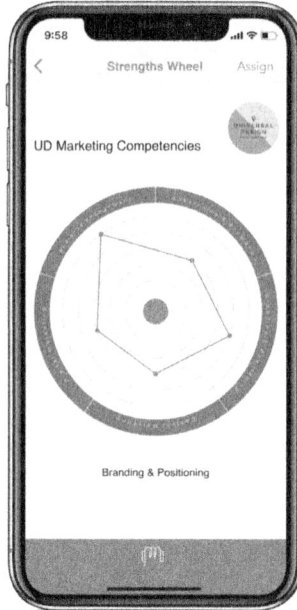

FIGURE 3.18 MasterCoach Strengths Wheel

Next, Wan uses MasterCoach to take notes while coaching, by launching the 'CoachPad'. He takes notes and tags action items, which will upload to the Dashboard for tracking progress and achievements (Figure 3.19).

FIGURE 3.19 MasterCoach CoachPad

Cheryl follows through with her action steps (Action Step 1: Complete Product Launch Proposal, Action Step 2: Engage a Public Relations Consultant) over the next couple of weeks. She updates her progress in the app and Wan gets real-time feedback on how she is doing (Figure 3.20).

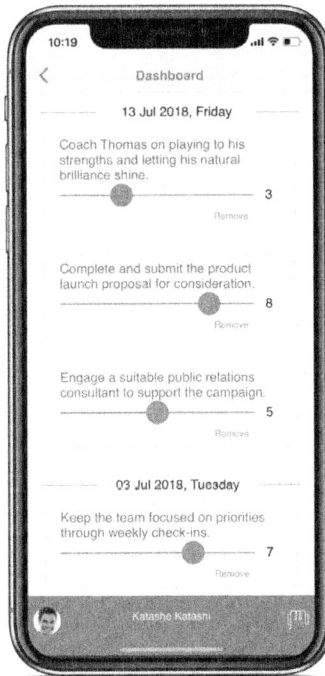

FIGURE 3.20   MasterCoach Dashboard

Source: Transcript from the online video demo of the MasterCoach app by 7M Consulting Private Limited (Singapore) – Exclusive owner of the MasterCoach App and Institute, and the MasterCoach 3D Coaching System

The actional phase: transfer to action

After having formulated a goal and an intention to implement specific actions to attain the goal, clients go on to execute their planned actions. One way for digital tools to support clients in implementing their intended goal-oriented actions is by keeping a record of their progress towards their goal. In addition, progress tracking offers the coach feedback on how their clients are progressing with their goals, and it allows the coach and clients' peers to offer encouragement and support between coaching sessions.

Using the software *Coachmetrix* for instance, coachees can invite their peers to follow their progress towards their set goals and to provide ongoing feedback, encouragement and suggestions. As another example, the *CoachAccountable* software includes among other features, metrics to track progress, an overview of clients' planned actions and it allows to send reminders (Box 3.14).

BOX 3.14 CASE EXAMPLE: PROGRESS TRACKING WITH COACHACCOUNTABLE

Greg is a sales coach. In one of his programs he coaches high-end management consultants to be effective sales people, a critical component of business development within consulting firms. Over an eight-week program Greg teaches them skill sets that are typically way outside of their comfort zone – sales mindset and strategy. Using CoachAccountable, Greg makes extensive use of metrics, having his coachees track KPIs around their sales funnel, as well as for building habits, like mastering elevator pitches and handling common objections for smoothness that only muscle memory can provide. CoachAccountable helps build those habits by routine metric reminders *('How many times did you practice your pitch today?'),* and as Greg puts it *'because they can just reply to the email reminder with their number, they actually do it'* (Figure 3.21).

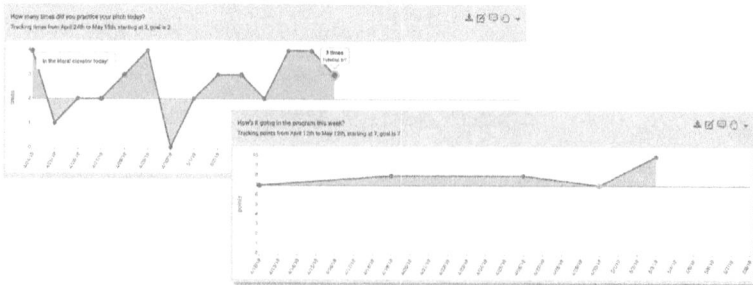

FIGURE 3.21   CoachAccountable (developer: John Larson)

At the end of the week, Greg has CoachAccountable set up to send a 'how's it going' survey to all his coachees, which effectively collects testimonials for him as well as lets coachees appreciate their own progress of what they got recently. In Greg's own words: *'It never works as well to ask them to take stock at the end of the program, they forget all of the progress and wins that happened earlier. This way they really appreciate the progress as they're making it'* (Figure 3.22).

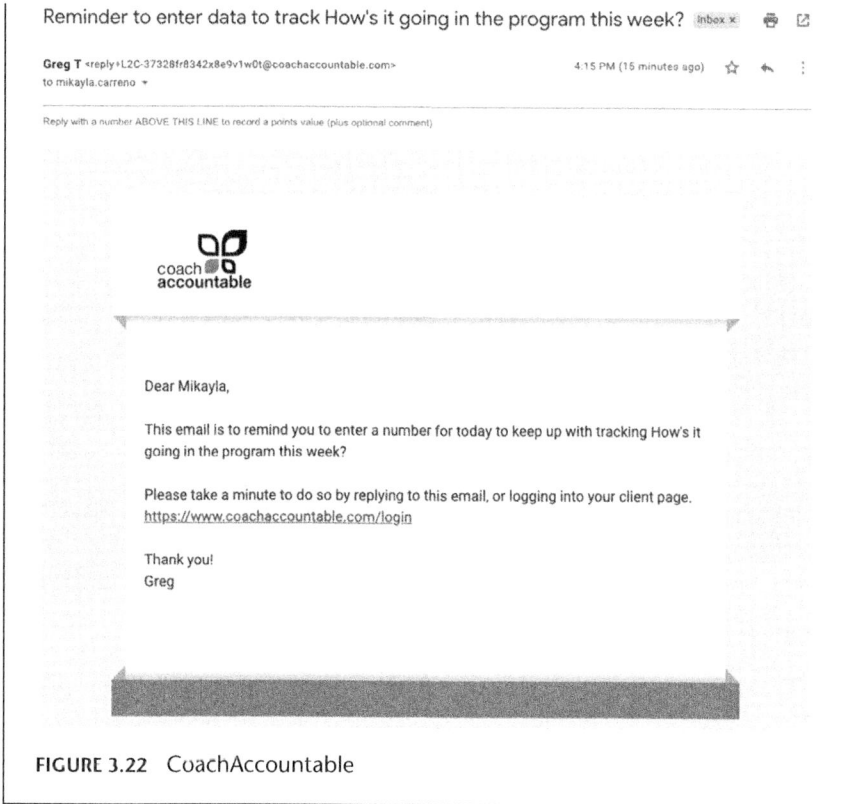

Reminder to enter data to track How's it going in the program this week? Inbox x 🖶 ☐

Greg T <reply+L2C-37328fr8342x8e9v1w0t@coachaccountable.com>   4:15 PM (15 minutes ago)   ☆ ↰ ⋮
to mikayla.carreno ▾

Reply with a number ABOVE THIS LINE to record a points value (plus optional comment)

coach◗◖
accountable

Dear Mikayla,

This email is to remind you to enter a number for today to keep up with tracking How's it going in the program this week?

Please take a minute to do so by replying to this email, or logging into your client page. https://www.coachaccountable.com/login

Thank you!
Greg

FIGURE 3.22   CoachAccountable

Several other tools enable progress tracking, among which are, *Achiiva, CoachingCloud®, CoachSimple, Goalify,* and *WorkOnIt*. Gamification approaches to motivate and encourage coaching clients can also be useful during the actional phase. For instance, with *The LearnScape*, coachees receive points every time they achieve a goal or they complete an exercise, which they can compare with the points of their peers.

Transfer processes for challenging coaching tasks

Whilst there may be simple coaching tasks and uncomplicated situations, where clients can set goals, and then go on to implement their planned actions and attain their goals, transfer into practice can sometimes be challenging, particularly if habits need to be changed, or unexpected obstacles, whether inner resistances or external barriers, prevent from implementing planned actions (Greif, 2011). In some cases, role play can be used to practice actions in the safety of a virtual environment (Greif, 2011), such as that offered by *ProReal, LPScocoon®*, or *TRI Cat Spaces*.

Shadowing is another useful, but cost-intensive coaching technique. Telephone shadowing (see Greif, 2012) offers a cost-effective alternative. Furthermore, the Virtual Transfer module of the *Virtual Coaching (VC)* tool supports clients' transfer of planned steps to practical implementation through a specific sequence of text-based coaching questions (Box 3.15).

BOX 3.15 CASE EXAMPLE: SUPPORTING TRANSFER INTO PRACTICE WITH THE VIRTUAL COACHING (VC) TOOL

In 2018–2019, the coaching, training, and consultancy SCREEN GmbH offered training to the employees of trading partners of a large German telecommunications company to help them improve their performance. To support transfer from training into practice, SCREEN GmbH used the digital coaching tool, Virtual Coaching (VC).

The challenge

The company wanted to provide effective transfer support to employees who received sales training, with measurable results (increase in sales). At the same time, they wanted to avoid the time resources and costs that onsite support would involve.

The solution

The Virtual Transfer Coaching (VTC) module of the Virtual Coaching (VC) tool was selected as a cost- and time-effective online solution to support the training transfer of 15 participants. Participants were offered online support for 3.5 months through the VTC tool, whilst a second project was carried out in 2018–2019 for another 3.5 months with 13 participants. The short form of the tool meant that it could be integrated in the daily work of the participants without spending too much of their time.

The results

In the first project, after having received the VTC coaching program, participants' performance significantly increased in four areas of competence. Specifically, based on their self-reports, their competence increased in terms of assessing their clients' needs, presenting offers, closing deals, and in terms of their expertise (Figure 3.23).

Coachees' self-perceived competence

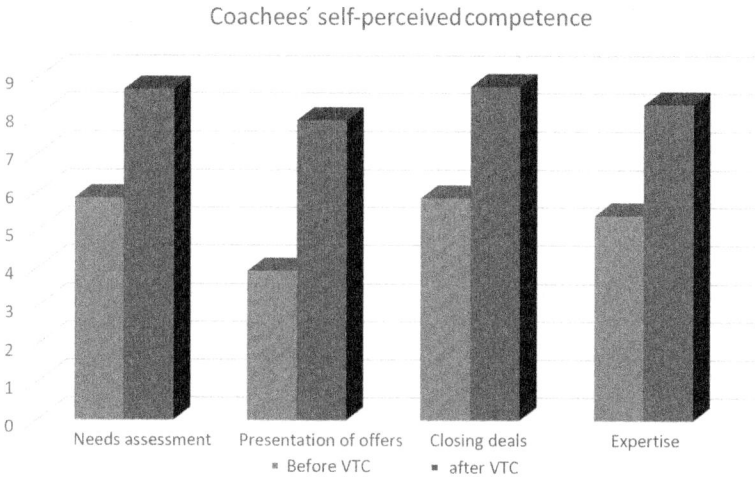

FIGURE 3.23 Four areas of competence perception before and after VTC, based on participants' self-reports

In the second project, the effectiveness that the VTC program had on participants' transfer from training into practice was evaluated based on their self-reports, as well as their supervisors' assessments. The results demonstrated an improvement of participants' performance in terms of the same four areas of competence (needs assessment, presentation of offers, closing deals, and expertise), based on their self-reports and their supervisors' ratings (Figure 3.24).

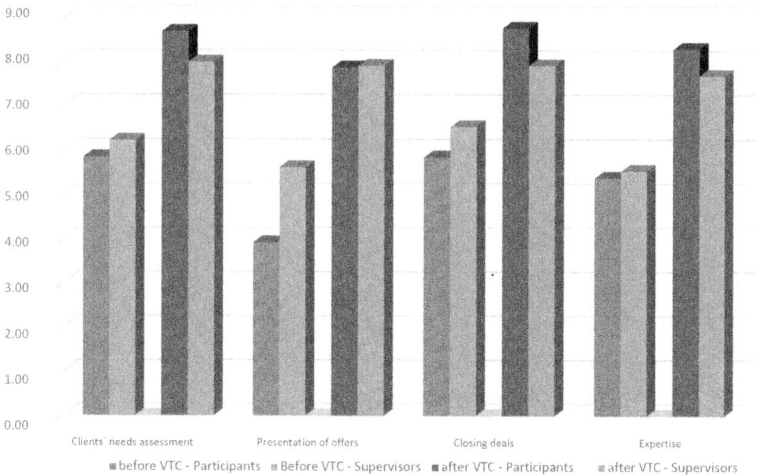

FIGURE 3.24 Four areas of competence perception before and after VTC, based on self-reports and supervisors' ratings

In comparison to a control group of participants' who had received the same training, but who hadn't used the VTC tool, the VTC pilot group improved their sales performance (Figure 3.25).

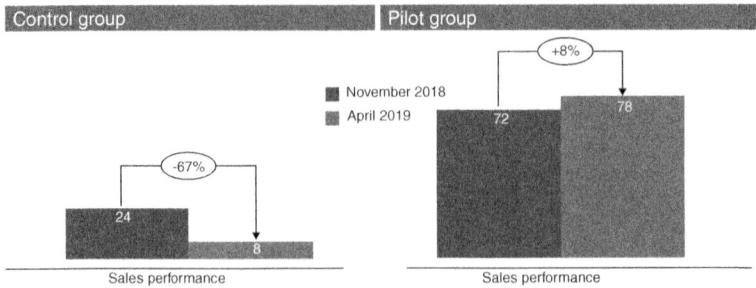

FIGURE 3.25   Difference between pilot and control groups in sales performance

When they were asked about the reason behind their sales performance improvement, participants of the pilot group attributed this improvement to the VTC program. Specifically, 62% of the participants expressed that without the VTC tool they wouldn't have attained their goals and they rated the VTC tool to have been very helpful for them (Figure 3.26).

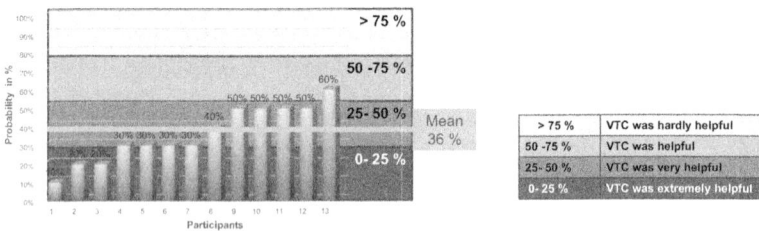

FIGURE 3.26   Participants' positive rating of VTC

The post-actional phase: evaluating the process

The post-actional phase involves clients' reflection on the coaching process, lessons learned that can be used in future situations, and process evaluation. Particularly, it is important for clients' self-monitoring and process evaluation, to analyse the actions that have been implemented to reach their goals or have failed to be implemented. Alternatives may need to be found if the planned actions haven't been successfully implemented and eventually goals may need to be redefined. Apart from the face-to-face, audio, video, or text-based communication, clients' reflection may be encouraged by asynchronous pre-structured coaching questions, such as those of the self-coaching module of the *Virtual Coaching* (VC) tool (see example in Box 3.16). Such questions guide clients to reflect on the process and to evaluate the extent to which, they successfully implemented their planned actions and attained their goals.

BOX 3.16 CASE EXAMPLE: PROCESS EVALUATION WITH THE QUESTIONS OF THE VIRTUAL SELF-COACHING (VSC) TOOL

1	*My goal-oriented steps of the last days*	*What facilitated the completion of the goal-oriented steps in the last days*
	• How many days am I looking back? • How important – expressed on a scale from 0 to 10 – was for me the practical implementation of the steps I planned? • What have I done specifically to come closer to my coaching goal (module 1)? • How difficult - expressed on a scale from 0 to 10 – was for me the implementation of these steps? (10 = possible, but only with great effort) • How well - expressed on a scale from 0 to 10 – have I completed these steps? (10 = perfect) • To what percentage have I achieved my coaching goal (module 1)? • What have I done specifically to come closer to my learning and developmental goal (module 2)? • How difficult - expressed on a scale from 0 to 10 – was for me the implementation of these steps? (10 = possible, but only with great effort) • How well - expressed on a scale from 0 to 10 – have I completed these steps? (10 = perfect) • To what percentage have I achieved my coaching goal (module 1)?	• Which was the most important factor in my environment that facilitated the completion of my goal-oriented steps in the last few days? • What is the most important action I carried out in the last few days, in order to optimally use this factor? • Which of my personality traits or capabilities facilitated the completion of my planned steps in the last few days? • What is the most important action I carried out in the last few days, in order to optimally use this capability or personality trait?
2	*What has prevented the completion of my planned steps in the last days*	*Observation of the right time for the completion of the planned steps*
	• Which is the most important factor in my environment that prevented the completion of my goal-oriented steps in the last few days? • What is the most important action I carried out in the last few days, in order to minimize this factor? • Which of my personality weaknesses prevented the completion of my planned steps in the last few days the most? • What is the most important action I carried out in the last few days, in order to overcome this challenge?	• How important – expressed on a scale from 0 to 10 – was for me the last days to observe the practical implementation of the steps I planned? (10 = extremely important) • Where exactly did I focus in the last days, in order to identify the right situation and favorable time for the completion of the planned goal – oriented steps? • How difficult was for me – expressed on a scale from 0 to 10 – this observation? (10 = can be completed, but with great effort) • How good – expressed on a scale from 0 to 10 – was my observation? (10 = perfect)
3	*Self-observation during completion of my goal-oriented steps in the next days (10 = can be completed, but with great effort)*	*Observing what happened after completion of my goal-oriented steps*
	• What exactly have I observed in myself in the last few days as I completed my planned goal-oriented steps? • How important was for me – expressed on a scale from 0 to 10 – this self-observation during carrying out these steps? • How difficult was for me – expressed on a scale from 0 to 10 – this self-observation? • How well – expressed on a scale from 0 to 10 – have I observed myself in the last few days? (10 = perfectly)	• How important was it for me – expressed on scale from 0 to 10 – to observe what happened after the completion of my goal-oriented steps? (10 – extremely important) • Where exactly did I focus in the last days to identify what happens after completion of my goal-oriented stpes • How difficult was for me – expressed on a scale from 0 to 10 – this observation? (10 = can be completed, but with great effort)

FIGURE 3.27   The Virtual Self-Coaching tool

An overview of purpose-built tools

As we've seen, some tools can accompany clients throughout the whole process, whilst other tools support clients during one specific coaching phase. An overview of the types of coaching-specific tools that can be used to support clients during the different phases of the coaching process is offered in Table 3.2.

Also, a single coaching-specific platform may consist of a combination of tool types. Table 3.3 provides a breakdown of various coaching-specific software currently available in the market according to the types of support they provide.

Furthermore, digital coaching tools differ from one another in several respects:

• **Content form**.

Coaching tools differ in terms of whether they support text-based, visual, audio, video, or multimedia content. Tools may consist of predominantly text, as it is the case with journaling tools and question sets, or visual content, such as virtual worlds and constellation tools, audio or video content, for instance, audio and video resources for reflection, or they may combine a mixture of different elements. Noting that many of the text-based tools may contain some pictorial content and vice versa, visual tools may include text.

• **Temporal use**.

Some tools are used real-time during the telephone, video, text-based, or face-to-face coaching conversation. Others are used asynchronously, in between coaching sessions or prior to the initial coaching session. Some tools support both, real-time and asynchronous modes of communication.

TABLE 3.2 Types of coaching-specific tools

		Motivational phase	*Volitional phase*	*Actional phase*	*Post-actional phase*
Mainly text-based	Reflective journals	✓	✓	✓	✓
	Pre-structured question sets	✓	✓	✓	✓
	Goal-setting tools	✓	✓		
Mainly visual	Progress tracking			✓	
	Assessments	✓	✓		
	Metaphorical images	✓	✓		
	Simulations	✓	✓		

TABLE 3.3 Coaching-specific tools

| | | Pre-structured content | | | | | | | | | | | Client data management (billing, scheduling sessions, dashboard) | |
		Journaling	AI-assisted	No AI	Problem analysis / Goal setting	Resource activation	Progress tracking	Assessments	Sharing resources	Images	Simulations	Action planning	Process evaluation		Matching
1	Achiiva	✓		✓	✓		✓					✓		✓	
2	Amanda		✓				✓	✓							
3	BRiN		✓				✓	✓	✓						
4	Butterfly		✓	✓			✓	✓							
5	CAI® Attentiveness Month app	✓		✓						✓					
6	CAI® Attentiveness Week app	✓		✓						✓					
7	CAI® Good Morning app	✓		✓	✓										
8	CAI® Problem-Solution app	✓		✓	✓										
9	CAI® Resource Tree app	✓		✓		✓									
10	CAI® Resource Wheel app					✓									
11	CAI® Scribo	✓			✓	✓	✓		✓			✓			
12	CAI® Silence and Strength app			✓	✓	✓							✓		

(Continued)

TABLE 3.3 (Cont.)

	Journaling	Pre-structured content		Problem analysis / Goal setting	Resource activation	Progress tracking	Assessments	Sharing resources	Images	Simulations	Action planning	Process evaluation	Client data management (billing, scheduling sessions, dashboard)	Matching
		AI-assisted	No AI											
CAI® Solution Finder			✓	✓	✓	✓			✓	✓				
13 CAI® Summer Forest app			✓	✓	✓	✓		✓	✓	✓	✓		✓	✓
14 CAI® Visualize Targets app			✓	✓										
15 CAI® World Platform			✓	✓	✓									
16 Charlie		✓												
17 CleverMemo	✓		✓				✓				✓			
18 CoachAccountable	✓					✓		✓					✓	
19 Coach Bot		✓				✓							✓	
20 Coaches Console						✓		✓					✓	
21 Coaching Cloud®						✓		✓					✓	✓
22 Coachfox	✓												✓	✓
23 CoachHub	✓					✓							✓	✓
24 Coaching Lobby						✓		✓						
25 CoachMaster™			✓	✓	✓	✓					✓			
26 Coachmetrix			✓	✓				✓			✓			

27	Coaching Moments
28	CoachSimple™
29	Coach Yourself
30	Coach Your Success
31	Cognitive Coaching^SM app
32	Cylient Coaching Moments®
33	Falcon Pro
34	7 Fields
35	Goalify
36	IBM Watson™ Career Coach
37	Insala
38	iThrive
39	Jigsawbox
40	JournalEngine™
41	LeaderAmp
42	Life Coach Hub
43	LPScocoon®
44	Mentornity
45	Orai
46	Pluform
47	Pluma
48	Pocket Confidant

(Continued)

TABLE 3.3 (Cont.)

	Journaling	Pre-structured content AI-assisted	Pre-structured content No AI	Problem analysis / Goal setting	Resource activation	Progress tracking	Assessments	Sharing resources	Images	Simulations	Action planning	Process evaluation	Client data management (billing, scheduling sessions, dashboard)	Matching
49 ProReal			✓	✓	✓					✓	✓			
50 Remente			✓	✓	✓						✓			
51 Satori													✓	
52 Skinio		✓		✓	✓			✓						
53 Sono VR			✓	✓	✓						✓			
54 Symblify			✓	✓	✓				✓		✓			
55 Tess		✓	✓	✓	✓									
56 The Coaching Tools Company		✓		✓	✓						✓			
57 The LearnScape			✓	✓	✓	✓					✓			
58 The MasterCoach app			✓	✓	✓	✓	✓				✓			
59 TypeCoach			✓	✓			✓	✓						
60 TriCat Spaces			✓	✓	✓			✓	✓		✓			
61 Virtual Coaching (VC)			✓	✓	✓			✓	✓	✓	✓			
62 Woebot		✓		✓	✓	✓					✓			
63 WorkOnIt			✓	✓	✓	✓								
64 Wysa		✓		✓	✓				✓					
65 Zurich Resource Model online tool (ZRM)			✓	✓										

- **Software type**.

Some of the available tools are web-based applications, and some of them mobile or iPad applications.

- **Content structure**.

Some tools are content-free authoring tools that allow coaches using the software to create their own coaching questions, assignments, or modules. Other tools consist of pre-structured content, such as predetermined coaching question sets, resources, and surveys. Some tools offer both predefined content and the option to create one's own content during the coaching process.

- **Interactivity**.

Most coaching tools offer interactive resources, whether it is typing in answers to coaching questions, or exploring virtual environments and manipulating virtual objects. A few of them are non-interactive, offering for instance, resources for the client to read or view.

- **Feature complexity**.

Coaching tools may have one main feature, for instance, written coaching questions, or they may integrate multiple capabilities, for instance, progress tracking, note taking, journaling, assessments, and questions.

- **Independence**.

Many of the available tools are used as add-ons, to support various coaching tasks, beyond the dialogue with the coach. Some tools are standalone, as they not only provide solutions for supporting various aspects of the coaching process (during or in between coaching conversations), and for managing client data including invoicing and scheduling sessions, but they also have a built-in audio, video, or text chat to facilitate the coaching conversation, all in one platform. Self-coaching tools are also standalone tools, in that the client–machine interaction takes place without the need to use other media and platforms to facilitate a dialogue (although the option is often given in such self-coaching programs).

- **Coach involvement**.

Coaching tools are designed to enhance coach-facilitated, or relational coaching engagements (coach–client interaction). Some tools are designed as self-coaching programs (client–machine interaction).

- **Theoretical background**.

Some tools, typically the authoring tools with no predefined content, are theoretically neutral. They can be integrated in the work of coaches from different backgrounds, approaches, and expertise. However, many of the available coaching-specific tools are bound to a coaching approach or model (e.g. cognitive-behavioural approach, systemic approaches, the GROW model, SMART, etc.). For instance, the platform *Pluform* uses the Accelerated Behavioural Change (ABC) model for coaching, which consists of three phases: The analysis phase is used to map coachees' current situation and to formulate clear coaching goals. The internalizing phase, during which coachees work closely with their coach towards achieving their goal and towards internalizing new behaviours or skills. In the final phase, the focus lies on ensuring the sustainability of coaching outcomes. Another tool that is linked with the behavioural approach to coaching is *Virtual Coaching (VC)*, which places strong emphasis on formulating specific and achievable goals. This tool is also based on a solution-oriented approach to help clients focus positively on their strengths and resources, set goals and work out how to achieve them. It has a clear focus on the present and future and uses methods, such as the miracle question and scaling questions to facilitate clients' progress towards their goals. *ProReal* on the other hand, uses elements of the psychodynamic approach, as clients can add for instance, head-like figures behind their avatar to represent their inner voice. The client's sub-egos are given a speech caption, colour, and size and can move behind the client's avatar.

- **Coaching context**.

Some tools are designed for business related issues, others for life coaching, or career coaching. Authoring tools such as reflective journaling tools can be used in any context.

- **Other features:**

  - **AI-based:** Some coaching tools are AI-assisted.
  - **Client data management**: Some tools support client data management, allowing the coach to maintain an overview of all interactions, data, past and scheduled sessions. They allow to schedule sessions and send invites to meetings.
  - **Branding:** Many coaching software allow the coach to use their own logo and brand.
  - **Matching**: Some tools allow coaches to set up a profile and facilitate the matching process between coaches and clients, according to specialization and level of expertise.
  - **Billing/invoicing**: Some tools include admin functions, such as billing and managing transactions.

Table 3.4 on pp. 98–105 offers examples of purpose-built tools based on these ten characteristics.

Out of 61 tools that were developed in the last 16 years, 51 tools were developed only in the last eight years. Even though this may not be an exhaustive list of the available tools, it gives an indication of the pace with which, new coaching platforms are recently being developed to meet the needs for flexible, scalable, time, and cost-efficient coaching.

The number of coaching-specific tools, including web and mobile applications and more recently, AI-assisted tools, is growing exponentially as technology matures (see Figure 3.28). Following the invention of the iPhone in 2007, numerous mobile apps for coaching have been developed in the last few years (see Figure 3.29), and the recent advances in Artificial Intelligence have fostered the development of several AI-powered coaching chatbots (see Chapter 4).

Differences between coaching-specific versus generic tools

Many coaching-specific tools serve similar purposes to generic tools. For instance, coaches may use Microsoft Word to take session notes, to incorporate journal entries or to ask the client to reflect and respond to sets of coaching questions, which leads to the question: what do we need coaching-specific software for? On the other hand, coaching-specific tools differ from generic tools in several respects:

- **Coaching methods and expertise**: Pre-structured coaching-specific tools tend to incorporate coaching models (e g GROW, SMART), coaching approaches and coaching expertise. Pre-set question frameworks incorporate coaching methods.

For instance, the tool *Pluform* is based on the Accelerated Behavioural Change (ABC) model, a three-phase coaching model that was developed by Ribbers and Waringa. The first phase focuses on mapping clients' current situation and identifying specific coaching goals. In the second phase, the focus lies on achieving their goal and towards internalizing new behaviours or skills. The third phase focuses on ensuring the sustainability of coaching outcomes.

The tool *Virtual Coaching (VC)* incorporates elements of the behavioural approach to coaching, which places strong emphasis on formulating specific and achievable goals. It is also based on a solution-oriented approach, as it supports clients in focusing on their strengths and positive resources, setting goals and working out how to achieve them. It has a clear focus on the present and future and uses methods, such as the miracle question and scaling questions to facilitate clients' progress towards their goals.

ProReal uses techniques based on Moreno's psychodrama. Clients may use props as visual metaphors, and they may add head-like figures behind their avatar to represent their inner voice. The clients' sub-egos are given a speech caption, colour, and size and can move behind the client's avatar.

CoachMaster™ follows the stages of the GROW model to support clients from goal setting through to defining action steps, and the mobile app *WorkOnIt*

TABLE 3.4 Coaching-specific tools based on ten characteristics

Tool name	Content form	Temporal use	Structure	Feature complexity	Interactivity	Independence	Coaching context	Coach involvement	Software type
Achiva	Text	Asynchronous	Authoring content	Multiple features	Interactive	Supporting tool	Life and business	Coach–led	Mobile application
Amanda	Text	Synchronous	Predefined content	Multiple features	Interactive	Standalone tool	Business coaching	Self-coaching	Mobile application
BRiN	Text and video	Asynchronous	Predefined content	Multiple features	Interactive	Supporting tool	Business coaching	Self-coaching	Mobile application
Butterfly	Text	Asynchronous	Pre-structured and authoring content	Multiple features	Interactive	Standalone tool	Business coaching	Self-coaching	Mobile application
CAI® Attentiveness Month app	Text	Asynchronous	Predefined content	Single feature	Interactive	Supporting tool	Life coaching	Self-coaching	Mobile application
CAI® Attentiveness Week app	Text	Asynchronous	Predefined content	Single feature	Interactive	Supporting tool	Life coaching	Self-coaching	Mobile application
CAI® Good Morning app	Audio and text	Asynchronous	Predefined content	Single feature	Interactive	Supporting tool	Life coaching	Self-coaching	Mobile application
CAI® Problem-Solution app	Audio and text	Asynchronous	Predefined content	Single feature	Interactive	Supporting tool	Life coaching	Self-coaching	Mobile application
CAI® Resource Tree app	Text	Asynchronous	Predefined content	Single feature	Interactive	Supporting tool	Life coaching	Self-coaching	Mobile application
CAI® Resource Wheel app	Text	Asynchronous	Predefined content	Single feature	Interactive	Supporting tool	Life coaching	Self-coaching	Mobile application

CAI® Resource Wheel app	Visual and text	Asynchronous use	Predefined content	Single feature	Interactive	Supporting tool	Life and business coaching	Coach-led	Mobile application
CAI® Scribo	Text	Asynchronous use	Predefined content	Single feature	Interactive	As standalone or as a supporting tool	Life and business coaching	Coach-led	Web application
CAI® Silence and Strength app	Audio and text	Asynchronous use	Predefined content	Single feature	Interactive	Supporting tool	Life and business coaching	Coach-led	Mobile application
CAI® Solution Finder app	Text and visual	Asynchronous use	Predefined content	Single feature	Interactive	Supporting tool	Life and business coaching	Coach-led	Mobile application
CAI® Summer Forest app	Audio and text	Asynchronous use	Predefined content	Single feature	Interactive	Supporting tool	Life and business coaching	Coach-led	Mobile application
CAI® Visualizing targets	Audio and text	Asynchronous use	Predefined content	Single feature	Interactive	Supporting tool	Life and business coaching	Coach-led	Mobile application
CAI® World	Audio-visual and text	Synchronous and asynchronous use	Predefined content	Multiple features	Interactive	Stand-alone tool	Business coaching	Coach-led	Web-based application
Charlie	Text	Asynchronous use	Predefined content	Single feature	Interactive	Stand-alone tool	Life coaching	Self-coaching	Web-based application
CleverMemo	Text	Asynchronous use	Authoring and predefined contents	Multiple features	Interactive	Supporting tool	Life/business coaching	Coach-led	Web-based application

(Continued)

TABLE 3.4 (Cont.)

Tool name	Content form	Temporal use	Structure	Feature complexity	Interactivity	Independence	Coaching context	Coach involvement	Software type
CoachAccountable	Text, visual	Asynchronous use	Authoring content	Multiple features	Interactive	Supporting tool	Business coaching	Coach-led	Web-based application
Coach Bot	Text	Asynchronous use	Predefined content	Multiple features	Interactive	Supporting tool	Business coaching	Self-coaching	Mobile application
Coaches Console	Text	Asynchronous use	Authoring content	Multiple features	Interactive	Supporting tool	Business coaching	Coach-led	Web-based application
Coaching Cloud®	Text	Synchronous and asynchronous use	Authoring content	Multiple features	Interactive	Stand-alone tool	Life and business coaching	Coach-led	Web-based application
Coachfox	Audio-visual and text	Synchronous	Authoring content	Single main feature	Interactive	Stand-alone tool	Life and business coaching	Coach-led	Web-based application
CoachHub	Audio-visual and text	Synchronous and asynchronous use	Authoring content	Multiple features	Interactive	Stand-alone tool	Business coaching	Coach-led	Web-based application
Coaching Lobby	Text	Asynchronous use	Authoring content	Multiple features	Non-interactive	Supporting tool	Life and business coaching	Coach-led	Web-based application
Coach Master™	Text	Synchronous and asynchronous use	Predefined content	Single feature	Interactive	Stand-alone or as a supporting tool	Life and business coaching	Coach-led	Web-based application

Coachmetrix	Text and visual	Asynchronous use	Authoring content	Multiple features	Interactive	Supporting tool	Business coaching	Coach-led	Web-based application
Coaching Moments	Text and visual	Asynchronous use	Authoring content	Single main feature	Interactive	Supporting tool	Business coaching	Self-coaching	Mobile application
Coach Simple™	Text and visual	Asynchronous use	Authoring content	Multiple features	Interactive	Supporting tool	Business coaching	Coach-led	Web-based application
Coach Yourself	Audio and text	Asynchronous use	Predefined content	Single main feature	Non-interactive	Supporting tool	Life coaching	Self-coaching	Mobile application
Coach Your Success	Text	Asynchronous use	Predefined content	Single main feature	Interactive	Supporting tool	Life coaching	Self-coaching	Mobile application
Cognitive Coaching^SM app	Text	Synchronous/asynchronous use	Authoring content	Single main feature	Interactive	Supporting tool	Life/business coaching	Coach-led	Mobile application
Cylient coaching moments® app	Text and audio	Asynchronous use	Predefined content	Single main feature	Interactive	Supporting tool	Life coaching	Self-coaching	Mobile application
Falcon Pro	Visual	Synchronous use	Pre-configured elements	One main feature	Interactive	Supporting tool	Business coaching	Coach-led	iPad/web-based application

(Continued)

TABLE 3.4 (Cont.)

Tool name	Content form	Temporal use	Structure	Feature complexity	Interactivity	Independence	Coaching context	Coach involvement	Software type
7Fields	Audio-visual, text	Synchronous/ asynchronous use	Authoring and predefined contents	One main feature	Interactive	Stand-alone tool	Business coaching	Coach-led	Web-based application
Goalify	Text and visual	Asynchronous use	Predetermined content	Multiple features	Interactive	Supporting tool	Life/business coaching	Self-coaching	Mobile application
IBM Watson™ Career Coach	Text	Asynchronous use	Predefined content	One main feature	Interactive	Stand-alone tool	Life (career) coaching	Self-coaching	Mobile application
insala	Text	Asynchronous use	Predefined content	Multiple features	Interactive	Supporting tool	Life and business coaching	Coach-led	Web-based application
Jigsawbox	Text	Asynchronous use	Predefined content	Single feature	Non-interactive	Supporting tool	Life coaching	Coach-led	Web-based application
JournalEngine™	Text	Asynchronous use	Authoring tool	One main feature	Interactive	Supporting tool	Life and business coaching	Coach-led	Web-based application
LeaderAmp	Text	Asynchronous use	Predefined content	Multiple features	Interactive	Supporting tool	Life and business coaching	Self-coaching	Mobile application
Life Coach Hub	Text	Asynchronous use	Pre-prepared modules	Multiple features	Interactive	Supporting tool	Life coaching	Coach-led	Web-based application

LPScocoon®	Visual	Synchronous use	Pre-configured elements	One main feature	Interactive	Supporting tool	Business coaching	Coach-led	Desktop application
Mentornity	Audio-visual, text	Synchronous and asynchronous use	Authoring tool	Multiple features	Interactive	Standalone tool	Business and life coaching	Coach-led	Web-based application
Orai	Text and visual	Synchronous	Predefined content	Single main feature	Interactive	Standalone tool	Business coaching	Self-coaching	Web-based application
Pluform	Mainly text	Synchronous and asynchronous use	Predefined content	Multiple features	Interactive	Stand-alone tool	Business coaching	Coach-led	Web-based application
Pluma	Audio-visual and text	Synchronous and asynchronous use	Predefined content	Multiple features	Interactive	Stand-alone tool	Business coaching	Coach-led	Web-based and mobile application
Pocket Confidant	Text	Synchronous use	Predefined content	Single feature	Interactive	Stand-alone tool	Life/business coaching	Self-coaching	Mobile application
ProReal	Visual	Synchronous use	Pre-configured elements	Single main feature	Interactive	Supporting tool	Business and life coaching	Coach-led	Desktop and iPad application
Remente	Visual and text	Asynchronous use	Pre-configured elements	Multiple features	Interactive	Supporting tool	Business and life coaching	Self-coaching	Mobile application
Satori	Text	Asynchronous use	Authoring tool	Single main feature	n/a	Supporting tool	Business and life coaching	For coach-led sessions	Web-based application

(Continued)

TABLE 3.4 (Cont.)

Tool name	Content form	Temporal use	Structure	Feature complexity	Interactivity	Independence	Coaching context	Coach involvement	Software type
Skimio	Visual, audio, text	Asynchronous use	Predefined content and authoring tool	Single main feature	Interactive	Supporting tool	Business coaching	Self-coaching	Mobile application
Sono VR	Visual	Synchronous use	Predefined content	Single main feature	Interactive	Supporting tool	Life coaching	Coach-led	Web-based application
Symblify®	Visual	Asynchronous use	Predefined content	Single main feature	Interactive	Supporting tool	Life coaching	Self-coaching	Mobile application
Tess	Text	Synchronous use	Predefined content	Single main feature	Interactive	Supporting tool	Life coaching	Self-coaching	Mobile application
The Coaching Tools Company	Text	Asynchronous use	Predefined content	Single main feature	Non-interactive	Supporting tool	Life coaching	Coach-led	Web-based application
The LearnScape	Mainly text	Asynchronous use	Predefined content and authoring tool	Multiple features	Interactive	Supporting tool	Business coaching	Coach-led	Desktop application
The MasterCoach	Text and visual	Asynchronous use	Predefined content and authoring tool	Multiple features	Interactive	Supporting tool	Business coaching	Coach-led	Mobile application
Thrive	Text	Asynchronous use	Predefined content	Single feature	Interactive	Supporting tool	Life, career coaching	Coach-led	Web-based application

	Medium	Use	Content	Features	Interactivity	Tool type	Coaching type	Coaching mode	Application
TypeCoach	Audio-visual, text	Asynchronous use	Predefined content	Single feature	Interactive	Supporting tool	Life, career coaching	Coach-led	Web-based application
TriCat Spaces	Audio-visual, text	Synchronous use	Pre-configured content	Multiple features	Interactive	Standalone tool	Business coaching	Coach-led	Desktop application
Virtual Coaching (VC)	Mainly text	Synchronous and asynchronous use	Pre-structured questions	Single main feature	Interactive	Supporting tool	Business and life coaching	Coach-led (it includes a coaching module for self-coaching)	Desktop application
Woebot	Text	Asynchronous use	Pre-structured questions	Single main feature	Interactive	Standalone tool	Life coaching	Self-coaching	Mobile application
WorkOnIt	Text	Asynchronous use	Pre-structured questions	Single main feature	Interactive	Standalone tool	Life and business coaching	Self-coaching	Mobile application
Wysa	Text	Asynchronous use	Pre-structured questions	Single main feature	Interactive	Standalone tool	Life coaching	Self-coaching	Mobile application
Zurich Resource Model online tool (ZRM)	Visual and text	Asynchronous use	Pre-structured questions	Single main feature	Interactive	Supporting tool	Life coaching	Self-coaching	Desktop application

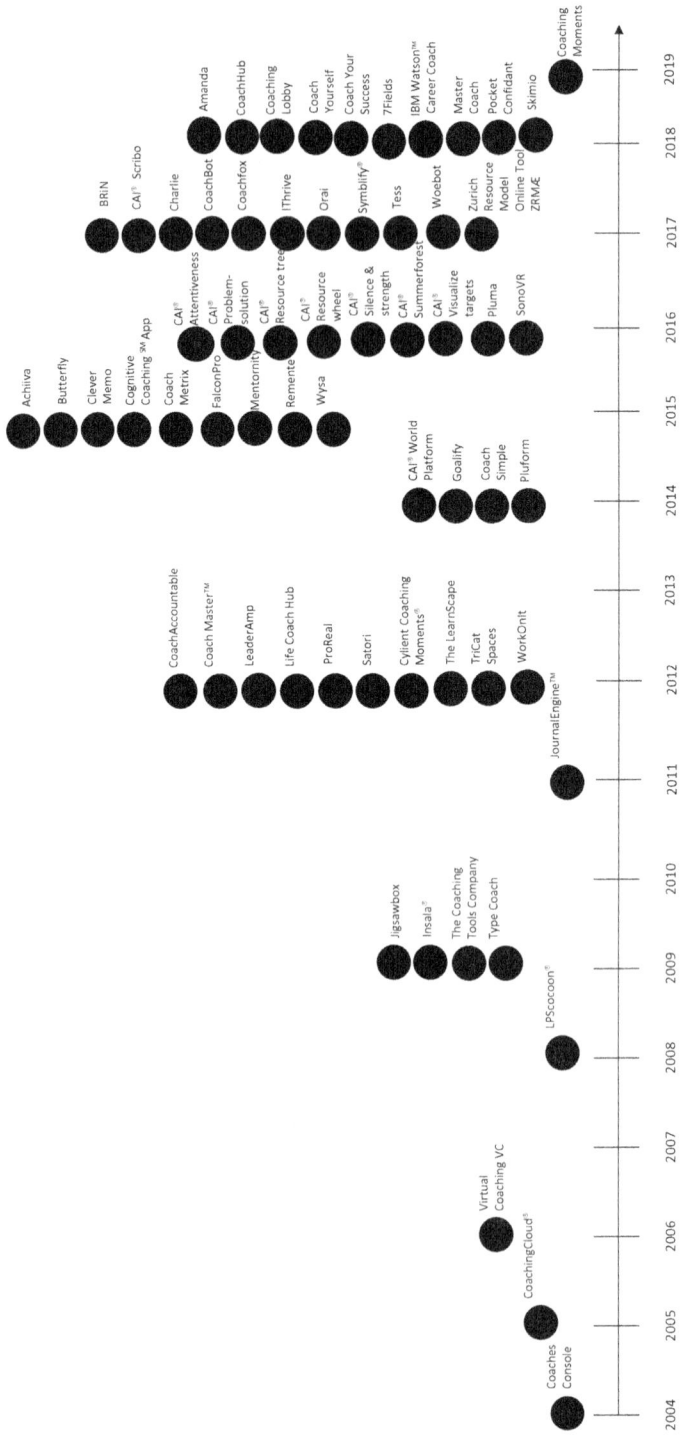

FIGURE 3.28 Timeline of coaching-specific tools 2004–2019

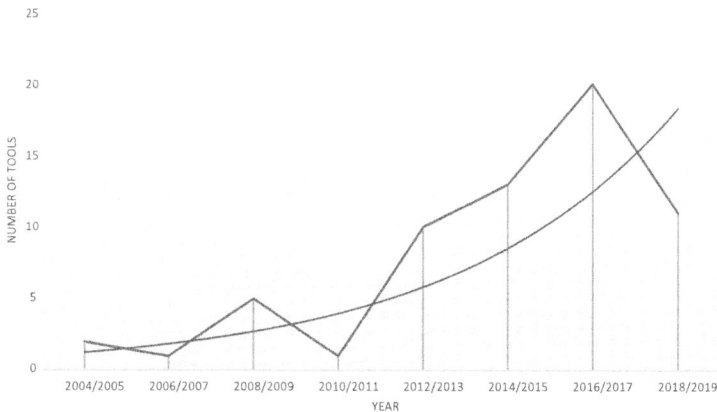

FIGURE 3.29   The increase of coaching-specific tools 2004–2019

is based on a SMART goals approach. The *Zurich Resource Model* online tool draws on a version of Heckhausen's (Heckhausen & Beckmann, 1990) and Gollwitzer's (1991) Rubicon Model, adapted by Grawe (1998, 2004).

- **Pre-structured content**: In contrast to generic tools, coaching-specific tools may contain pre-structured contents, offering a didactic structure (Geißler, 2008), which can be used to guide the coaching client's problem-solving process. Such tools may for instance, provide question sequences designed to stimulate clients' reflection and to use them as a basis for the verbal coaching conversation. They can be used during the conversation, or to guide clients between sessions, or in self-coaching programs. Such tools can be helpful for clients to work stepwise towards solving their problem and it can teach them problem-solving skills, which they can transfer to future situations for coaching themselves.
- **Coaching content storage and distribution**: Unlike generic tools, many purpose-built tools allow coaches to create and store contents, which can then be used by other coaches and clients. For instance, the *JournalEngine*, *CoachMaster*™, *Insala*®, and *Coaching Cloud* software all allow coaches to create their own coaching modules, which they can then store in the platform and offer them to their clients.
- **Encryption**: Unlike many generic tools, a lot of the available coaching software are encrypted, which makes them secure platforms of communication and allows secure data storage. Rather than using email to send clients coaching contents, coaching software often incorporate a secure mailing function.
- **All-in-one solutions**: In some cases, purpose-built tools combine several coaching tools, as well as capabilities to manage client data, billing, scheduling appointments and quite often they integrate one or more channels of

communication, e.g. audio, video, or text chat. Such tools provide all-in-one, standalone solutions for managing and carrying out, not online an entire coaching process, but all of the coach's clients and processes in one platform.

- **Branding**: Often purpose-built tools (e.g. CoachAccountable, Jigsawbox, JournalEngine™, Insala®, Life Coach Hub, Mentornity, Satori) allow coaches to customize the branding using their own logo design.

Coaching-specific tools: weaknesses and risks

Coaching-specific tools are not a panacea and even though they may support coaching processes, they can certainly not guarantee successful coaching outcomes.

Some coaching-specific tools could make the coaching conversation feel like a prescription. De Haan (2015) has warned against pre-coaching assessments, such as psychometric self-assessments and behavioural feedback instruments, which may not only not be helpful, but also they might even prevent clients from finding their own answer:

> Diagnostics are used 'on' the client, while coaching is the client using us, or at least client and coach wondering together what might be going on. Diagnostics impose a language on the client, while coaching inquires into the client's language when the client is really free to talk.
>
> *(De Haan, 2015, p. 16)*

Some of the available tools might oversimplify the coaching process and limit its complexity to a set of tasks to complete, ticking off a box after each task is carried out. For instance, the tool might ask: 'describe your problem – set your goal – write down your progress so far – and tick the box, when the goal is completed'. As we know however, it's not as simple as that. A lot depends on the skill of the coach, on the relationship between coach and client, or on external factors. Problem analysis and goal setting requires clients to reflect on their motives and needs, and on guidance in setting a concrete and realistic goal in relation to overcoming an existing problem. It is a process rather than a task. Whilst it's useful to document the problem and the defined goals in the system, or to write down reflections as a preparation for the coaching session, clients need more than just to respond to the software's prompt to 'describe the problem and set a goal'. In many cases, they might not be completely clear about where the problem lies and what the goal is at the beginning of the coaching process (Schein, 1999). Dialogue with the coach is necessary to clarify the underlying issue before being able to set goals. Or the goals that are set in the beginning of the coaching might need to be revised along the process. Therefore, predefined generic questions in a software might not always help to get down to the real issue.

In this sense, coaching software alone can make the coaching process feel mechanical and they might reduce its complexity to a set of tasks, incapable of fully capturing clients' issue and insufficient for providing meaningful solutions. Ticking off boxes after answering the questions in the software, doesn't necessarily mean that the desired coaching outcomes have been reached. Unexpected issues could arise, such as that actions towards attaining a defined goal are unsuccessful. Emotional barriers, habitual patterns, or interpersonal problems for instance, could get in the way. We may wish to change, but change is not always so easy to implement (Greif, 2011).

Coaching-specific tools should have a theoretical basis. Even though theoretical neutrality is not a risk in itself – after all, generic tools are also not based on a theory – the role of coaching-specific tools is typically more than recommending relevant resources to coachees. Coaching-specific tools may guide the coaching process, they may ask reflexive questions and they can be used to structure the coaching conversation. If they are not based on theory and scientific evidence, it's unlikely they can provide a good structure and guide the coaching client to attaining their goal. The risk is that whilst digital coaching comes at a reduced cost, the compromised quality of such tools create the image of a cheap and ineffective version of traditional coaching.

Predefined questions might also not cover all the different types of coaching issues. Coaching is not based on a doctor–patient model (Schein, 1999) and on making a diagnosis and prescribing a solution, it's about co-constructing meaning. Knowledge is jointly created and it requires reflexivity by both, the client and the coach. There can't be a 'one question fits all issues'. Instead different question frameworks should be developed to account for different types of issues.

In using coaching tools, whether generic or coaching-specific, the role of the coach is crucial. It is important for coaches and for coachees to be aware of the potential and the quality of the different tools that enter the market. Coaches need to be trained in using tools and the tools should augment the coaching, not limit it.

Recommendations for coaching software design

The landscape of coaching tools described in this chapter is changing constantly. It is certain that by the time this book is published, new tools will have entered the scene and perhaps some of the existing tools will have been replaced. Based on the types of coaching tools available, a lot can be said to improve the design of coaching software in the future.

Firstly, as discussed in the previous section, it is important for pre-structured coaching-specific tools to be theoretically founded, if they are to be truly useful in accompanying the client along the coaching process. They should incorporate theoretical models that will assist the coaching pair along the process of analysing the problem and identifying goals, to setting actions and implementing them, and to achieving the desired change. Theoretical models that cover all these phases, including the implementation of actionable steps, such as the Rubicon model (see Greif, 2011), could be helpful frameworks for new coaching tools to structure the coaching process (Geißler, 2018).

Secondly, the design of coaching software should take usability into account. In designing new tools, the developments in HCI and software design can be used to improve the coach's and client's experience. Over recent years, we've witnessed several changes in computer interfaces and in the way these interfaces allow us to interact with computers. For instance, while Command Line Interfaces are efficient, but require advanced computer users or system administrators, Graphical User Interfaces have allowed users to interact with graphical icons via keyboard and mouse and later, through touchscreens and thereby, have provided an easier way of interacting with computers. Machines are becoming more natural and intuitive. We have seen developments from using a keyboard to using touchscreens, and more recently to gesture recognition. The later developments in HCI include conversational interfaces (chatbots and voice assistants), gesture recognition and eye tracking technologies. These later developments potentially offer a new paradigm in UI, as these technologies mimic how we interact with the physical world, thereby leading to even more natural interactions with computers.

So far, there are several tools that can be accessed on the desktop, but also on mobile devices, increasing the possibilities to interact in a more intuitive way with them. This trend is likely to increase further as many ultrabooks offer touchscreen options. AR and VR technologies (to be discussed in the following chapter) also have the potential to enhance intuitive interaction and to overcome some of the barriers of using the mouse and keyboard, allowing a more embodied way of interacting with the computer. As these technologies involve sensors for tracking hand movement, eye and head movement, users interact with the computer by moving naturally, and in many cases by doing the same movement as they would if they were to perform the task in real life. For immersive VR, a lightweight HMD, high frame rates and comfort locomotion options such as vignetting and teleporting can eliminate cybersickness and offer a more embodied experience. Several virtual worlds similar to Second Life have already become available as immersive VR applications. Interaction with immersive VR environments means for instance, turning one's head to look around and physically reaching out to grab a virtual object, rather than having to learn which key to press. Coaching-specific desktop virtual reality applications could offer a significant improvement in coachees' experience, if they became compatible with immersive VR. Of course, such improvements would need to be weighed with the associated costs for development. Nevertheless, as with every technology costs are likely to continue to decrease over time.

The learnability of coaching tools can also be improved. For instance, the desktop-based Second Life may be seen as too complex to operate by many. To teleport for instance, the coachee needs to hold down Shift and press the key x. A certain learning curve is involved in navigating in a Second Life world, before figuring out what key does what and being able to easily move around. The design of similar coaching-specific tools could take this challenge into account and offer simple and clear navigation control paths. To improve the learnability of coaching tools, operating the system should be easy for users. Learnability is perhaps one of the barriers to using VR (desktop and immersive). Again, this may be changing as HMDs such as the Oculus Quest are becoming simple and easy to use.

References

Andrews, A. R. (2014). *Avatar coaching: A case study on the perceptions of virtual reality coaching interventions with an avatar coach.* Unpublished doctoral dissertation, Capella University, USA.

Cuddy, A. (2012). *Your body language may shape who you are.* TEDGlobal 2012, Retrieved from: www.ted.com/talks/amy_cuddy_your_body_language_shapes_who_you_are?language=en.

Damasio, A. (1994). *Descartes Irrtum – Fühlen, Denken und das menschliche Gehirn.* München: List Taschenbuch.

De Haan, E. (2015). Diagnostic tools in executive coaching – More harm than good? *Coaching Today,* July 2015, pp. 16–17.

Gassmann, D. & Grawe, K. (2006). General change mechanisms: The relation between problem activation and resource activation in successful and unsuccessful therapeutic interactions, *Clinical Psychology & Psychotherapy,* 13 (1), 1–11.

Geißler, H. (Ed.) (2008). *E-Coaching: Grundlagen der Berufs- und Erwachsenenbildung.* Baltmannsweiler: Schneider.

Geißler, H. (2018). State of the Art technikbasierter Medien im Coaching und in Coachingausbildung. Coaching Meets Research: Organisation, Digitalisierung und Design. Presentation at the 5th International Coaching Congress, Olten, 12/13 June 2018.

Geißler, H. (in press). *Coaching: Methodische Gestaltung elektronischer Coachingmedien.* Hamburg: Studienbrief, Hamburger Fern-Hochschule (HFH).

Geißler, H., Hasenbein, M., Kanatouri, S., & Wegener, R. (2014). E-coaching: Conceptual and empirical findings of a virtual coaching programme. *International Journal of Evidence Based Coaching and Mentoring,* 12 (2), 165–187.

Gollwitzer, P. M. (1991). *Abwägen und Planen: Bewußtseinslagen in verschiedenen Handlungsphasen* (Deliberating and planning: Mindsets in different action phases). Goettingen: Hogrefe.

Gollwitzer, P. M. (1999). Implementation intentions: Strong effects of simple plans. *American Psychologist,* 54 (7), 493–503.

Grabow, C. (2013). *LPScocoon®: A virtual constellation tool to enhance e-coaching.* Online resource. Retrieved from: https://digitalcoach.home.blog/2013/05/30/lpscocoon-a-virtual-constellation-tool-to-enhance-e-coaching/.

Grant, A. M. (2006). An integrative goal-focused approach to executive coaching. In D. Stober & A. M. Grant (Eds.), *Evidence-based coaching handbook: Putting best practices to work for your clients* (pp. 146–165). New York: Wiley.

Grawe, K. (1998). *Psychologische Psychotherapie.* Göttingen: Hogrefe.

Grawe, K. (2004). *Neuropsychotherapie.* Göttingen: Hogrefe.

Gray, D. E. (2007). Facilitating management learning: Developing critical reflection through reflective tools. *Management Learning*, 38 (5), 495–517.

Greif, S. (2008). *Coaching und ergebnisorientierte Selbstreflexion*. Göttingen: Hogrefe.

Greif, S. (2011). Goal and implementation intentions and their complex transfer into practice. In D. Megginson & D. Clutterbuck (Eds.) *Goal-break: The coach's or mentor's antidote to the tyranny of goal-setting*. Available online at: www.home.uni-osnabrueck.de/sgreif/downloads/Implementation_intentions.pdf

Greif, S. (2012). Telefon-Shadowing. Institut für wirtschaftspsychologische Forschung und Beratung, GmbH.

Greif, S. (2016). Putting goals to work in coaching: The complexities of implementation. In S. David, D. Clutterbuck, & D. Megginson (Eds.) *Beyond goals: Effective strategies for coaching and mentoring* (pp. 125–150). Oxford and New York: Routledge.

Griffiths, R. (2017). What new mentors really think about – And how to help. Actual e-coaching session – Part 1. Online resource Retrieved from: www.linkedin.com/pulse/what-new-mentors-really-think-how-help-actual-part-1-griffiths/.

Hancock, B. (2014). *The design of a framework and instrument for assessment of virtual coaching competence: An exploratory study*. Master's thesis, Stellenbosch University, South Africa.

Heckhausen, H. & Beckmann, J. (1990). Intentional action and action slips. Psychological Review, 97(1), 36–48.

Henderson, K., Napan, K., & Monteiro, S. (2004). *Encouraging reflective learning: An online challenge*. January 2014, Retrieved from: www.researchgate.net/publication/254743104_Encouraging_reflective_learning_An_online_challenge.

Huss, J. & Eichenberg, C. (2018). Serious Games und ihre Anwendung im Coaching. *Organisationsberatung, Supervision, Coaching*, 25 (3), 321–335.

Kanatouri, S. (2018). *Mapping the technology-assisted coaching field through the lens of an online community: An exploratory research*. Doctoral dissertation, Helmut-Schmidt Universität, Hamburg.

Schein, E. H. (1999). *Process Consultation revisited – Building the helping relationship*. Reading, MA: Addison-Wesley Publishing Inc.

Schmidt, F. & Thamm, A. (2008). *Wirkungen und Wirkfaktoren im Coaching. – Verringerung von Prokrastination und Optimierung des Lernverhaltens bei Studierenden*. Diplom thesis, Work and Organizational Psychology Unit, University of Osnabrück, Germany.

Schreyögg, A. (Ed.) (1995). *Coaching: Eine Einführung für Praxis und Ausbildung* (1st edition). Frankfurt and New York: Campus Verlag.

Schreyögg, A. (Ed.) (2012). *Coaching: Eine Einführung für Praxis und Ausbildung* (7th edition). Frankfurt and New York: Campus Verlag.

Storch, M. (2004). Crossing your personal rubicon. *Scientific American*, 14 (5), 32–33.

Tinker, D. (2013). *Remote coaching using virtual reality*. Online resource Retrieved from: https://digitalcoach.home.blog/2013/06/09/remote-coaching-using-virtual-reality/#more-50.

Torres, C., Brodnick, R., & Powel, D. (2009). In Focus: Virtual Learning – Leader development gets a second life. *Leadership in Action*, 29 (3), San Fransisco, Wiley.

Websites

1. Achiiva www.achiiva.com/
2. Butterfly www.butterfly.ai/
3. BRiN https://brin.ai

4. CAI® Attentiveness Week app https://play.google.com/store/apps/details?id=com.cai_world.caiattentivenessweek&hl=de

5. CAI® Attentiveness Month app https://play.google.com/store/apps/details?id=com.cai_world.caiattentivenessmonth&hl=de

6. CAI® Good Morning app https://play.google.com/store/apps/details?id=com.cai_world.goodmorning

7. CAI® Problem Solution app https://play.google.com/store/apps/details?id=com.cai_world.caisolveproblems&hl=en_IN

8. CAI® Resource Tree app https://play.google.com/store/apps/details?id=com.caiworld.cairesourcetree&hl=de

9. CAI® Resource Wheel app https://play.google.com/store/apps/details?id=com.cai_world.cairesourcewheel&hl=de_CH

10. CAI® Silence and Strength app https://play.google.com/store/apps/details?id=com.cai_world.silenceandstrength&hl=nl

11. CAI® Scribo www.cai-world.com/scribo

12. CAI® Sommer Forest app https://play.google.com/store/apps/details?id=com.cai_world.summerforest&hl=es_PY

13. CAI® World Platform www.cai-world.com/

14. CAI® Visualize Targets https://play.google.com/store/apps/details?id=com.cai_world.reachtargets&hl=de

15. CoachAccountable www.coachaccountable.com/

16. CoachApp24 www.coaching-akademie-muenchen.de/die-akademic/coaching-app/

17. CoachBot www.saberr.com/coachbot

18. Coaching Cloud® www.coachingcloud.com/

19. Coaches Console www.coachesconsole.com/

20. Coachfox https://coachfox.com/en/

21. CoachHub https://coachhub.io/en/home/

22. Coaching Lobby www.coachinglobby.com/

23. CoachMaster™ https://thecoachmasternetwork.com/coachmaster-network/

24. Coach.me www.coach.me/

25. Coachmetrix https://coachmetrix.com/

26. Coaching Moments https://coachingmoments.us/

27. Coach Simple™ www.coachsimple.net/

28. Coach Yourself www.coachyourself.com/

29. Coach Your Success https://coach-your-success.de/

30. Cognitive Coaching^{SM} app www.thinkingcollaborative.com/cognitive-coaching-app/

31. Cylient Coaching Moments® www.cylient.com/services/coaching-moments-app/

32. Falcon *pro* www.christian-bachler.com/de/falcon-pro

33. 7Fields www.7fields.io/

34. Goalify https://goalifyapp.com/en/reach-your-goals/

35. IBM® Watson™ Career Coach: www.ibm.com/talent-management/career-coach
36. Insala® www.insala.com/
37. Jigsawbox www.jigsawbox.com/
38. JournalEngine™ https://journalengine.com/
39. LeaderAmp www.leaderamp.com/
40. Life Coach Hub™ www.lifecoachhub.com/
41. LPScocoon® www.lpscocoon.de/
42. MasterCoach www.mastercoachapp.com/
43. Mentornity https://mentornity.com/
44. Orai www.orai.com/
45. Pluform www.pluform.com/en/
46. Pluma www.pluma.co/
47. PocketConfidant https://pocketconfidant.com/
48. ProReal www.proreal.world/
49. Remente www.remente.com/
50. Satori http://satoriapp.com/
51. Skimio https://skimio.com/
52. Sono VR http://sonovr.com/
53. Symblify™ www.symblify.net/
54. Tess www.x2ai.com/
55. The Coaching Tools Company www.thecoachingtoolscompany.com/
56. The LearnScape https://thelearnscape.com/
57. Thrive http://sonovr.com/
58. TriCAT Spaces www.tricat.net/tricat-spaces/
59. TypeCoach https://type-coach.com/
60. Virtual Coaching (VC) www.virtuelles-coaching.com/
61. Woebot https://woebot.io/
62. WorkOnIt http://workonit.coachbyapp.com/
63. Zurich Resource Model ZRM® online tool https://zrm.ch/zrm-online-tool-englisch/

4

EMERGING PERSPECTIVES

Immersive Virtual Reality

In the previous chapter, we looked at virtual environments, such as Second Life and
ProReal, as examples of desktop-based Virtual Reality applications that can be used
to enhance coaching processes. These desktop-based virtual worlds allow coaching
clients to visualize and express their coaching issue, and to simulate solutions in
a safe environment before implementing actions in the physical world. They often
involve avatars as representations of oneself, and symbolic objects that can be used
as visual metaphors for one's perceived obstacles and current situation.

Immersive Virtual Reality technology takes such experiences to another level,
as it allows the client to enter as part of the virtual environment and physically
interact with it, rather than looking at it and experiencing it through the confines
of a computer screen. Users can view objects in real-scale, and they may be able
to change their size from very small to very large, as well as to move and to rotate
objects, and to walk around them or even inside them (e.g. inside a ship or
a building). Today's consumer-ready VR technology uses a stereoscopic Head
Mounted Display (HMD) and hand controllers for tracking your hands and allowing detailed interaction and haptic feedback. The sensors built in the hardware
allow head and hand motion tracking, which contribute towards making the Virtual Reality environment feel realistic, or immersive to the user.

The evolution of immersive Virtual Reality technology

Immersive Virtual Reality (iVR) is not a new technology. The technology emerged
in the 1960s, when filmmaker Morton Heilig created the Sensorama (1962), an
arcade-style theatre cabinet that was used to simulate the senses. The Sensorama displayed stereoscopic 3D images, it included a vibrating seat and it generated a scent. In
1968, the computer scientist Ivan Sutherland created the first Head Mounted Display,

called the 'Sword of Damocles'. The device was a mechanical hand that was suspended from the ceiling and placed a screen in front of the user. It used stereoscopy, a technique for creating an illusion of depth in images and thereby enabling the view of 3D images. Even though the Sword of Damocles was an innovation and it paved the path for today's Head Mounted Display devices, the limited processing power of computers at that time, and the primitiveness and heavy weight of the device prevented it from providing a fully immersive experience. Over the years, Virtual Reality technology evolved, but due to its high cost and complexity it didn't see wide application, aside from the military and aerospace sectors. In the 1980s and the 1990s, flight simulators were developed for the military and training simulators for NASA. Over the last three decades, Virtual Reality has also been used for exposure therapy to help soldiers with PTSD, as well as for surgical training.

It is only recently however, that iVR became commercially available to consumers, with a significant decrease in cost, and significantly improved capabilities. A major breakthrough came along with the rapid democratization of the smartphone about ten years ago and the associated commoditization of high-resolution screens and sensors. The American entrepreneur Palmer Luckey took these rapidly improving and rapidly cheapening parts of phones and created the Oculus Rift, which was launched via the global crowdfunding platform Kickstarter in 2012 (Kickstarter was itself part of the breakthrough to get the idea exposed to many people). The Oculus Rift used the accelerometers and high-resolution lightweight screens from phones. The new Head Mounted Display was more affordable, and it offered lower latency tracking than anything else thus far on the market. Low latency tracking meant that there is an imperceptible delay between the head movement and the images displayed in the HMD, making the experience more believable.

In 2016 the consumer version of the Oculus Rift became available, with the HTC Vive HMD being launched a day later and Sony PSVR shortly after that. In the years that followed, the prices of HMDs reduced significantly, the technology continued to improve (e.g. inside-out tracking was perfected for HMDs), and mobile standalone HMDs with no separate phone or PC needed, were also recently released (e.g. the Oculus Quest). Roll forward to 2019 and the next generation of HMDs are launched with further significant breakthroughs:

- Improved displays, specifically higher resolutions than before (text was hard to read on the first generation HMDs, whereas the new ones have 40–80% higher resolutions) and a lower screen door effect (i.e. less black space between pixels, thus a better picture quality).
- Wider Field of View (FOV), i.e. the range of what the user can see (from 110° in 2016, some professional HMDs today have 160°–180°).
- Eye tracking, which offers a new way to interact whilst in VR, and enables foveated rendering, i.e. rendering in high resolution only directly where the user is looking, but everything else is rendered at a lower resolution.
- Mobile-based HMDs (such as the Oculus Quest and the Lenovo Mirage) have now reached the point that they can have full six Degrees of Freedom (DoF) tracking with six DoF hand controllers, meaning a great range of movement allowed and higher immersion for the user.

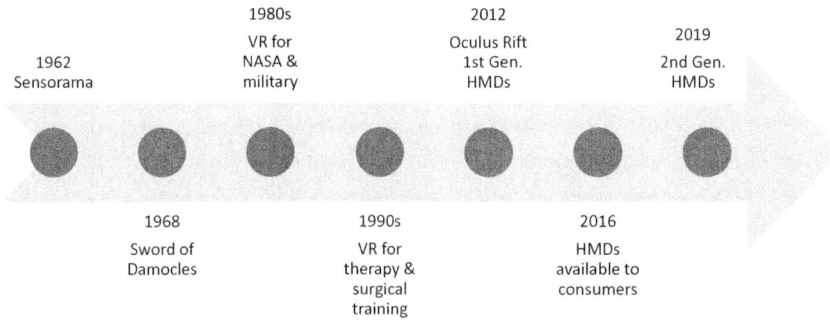

FIGURE 4.1 The evolution of immersive Virtual Reality

Immersion and presence

Since its early days, the goal of Virtual Reality technology has been immersion. Immersion is of course not unique to VR applications. We can be immersed in, or feel absorbed in other environments, for instance, in a virtual world that we view on our desktop, or in the narrative of a book or a film. Immersion may be defined as the extent of providing an illusion of reality (Slater & Wilbur, 1997). Slater and Wilbur (1994) distinguished *immersion*, which refers to the capability of the technology to create an illusion of reality, from *(spatial) presence*, a subjective psychological state, where one has the sense of physically being in the virtual environment. Research has indicated a correlation between immersion and presence, as several studies (e.g. Axelsson et al., 2001; Freeman et al., 2005; Havranek et al., 2012; Hoffman et al., 2003) assessing different aspects of immersion found higher presence in more immersive VR set-ups.

Immersion has different extents, with desktop VR providing lower immersion levels and iVR technology providing higher levels of immersion. Even though we may feel absorbed in a virtual environment that we experience on our desktop just like we may be absorbed in a film or a book, desktop VR technology is less immersive than iVR for several reasons, as described below. According to Slater and Wilbur (1994, p. 3) immersion in a virtual environment depends on its:

- *Inclusiveness*: an inclusive virtual environment is one in which, physical reality is occluded (as it is the case with HMD). In desktop-based VR, one can still look around and see their physical environment, and physical movement is not involved apart from finger clicks.
- *Extensiveness*: when several sensory modalities are accommodated (iVR supports visual feedback, stereoscopic sound, and some tactile feedback).
- *Surrounding view*: when the view is panoramic with a high Field of View (FoV) – in iVR the FoV is 180°, allowing us to see more of the VE at a time, and to make free head and body movements to see other parts of the VE.

- *Vividness*: the representational fidelity, i.e. the degree of realism, and pixel resolution.
- *Matching*: requires that there is a match between a user's feedback about body movement and information generated on the display, e.g. if I turn my head it will result in an immediate change of display.
- *Egocentric perspective (Virtual Body)*: the self-representation from an egocentric, first person perspective rather than a third person perspective. Desktop-based VR however, also allows both perspectives, first and third person. In addition, iVR users can move their head and body, and they may be able to look down and see their own (virtual) hands, making the egocentric perspective more realistic.

Moreover, iVR offers two important capabilities that are unique to it: Firstly, depth perception, which allows the perception of distance between objects (e.g. looking at an object and having a sense for how far away it is and whether we can reach it) and viewing them in 3D, and secondly scale, which allows to experience objects and environments in their true scale, or any other scale desired (for instance, to make them very small or very large). Interaction with the virtual environment is done in more natural ways than computer clicks, allowing embodied activity, such as grabbing objects, making hand gestures, using body language, and looking around.

As discussed, immersive VR technology enables the experience of realistic virtual environments, and thereby an illusion of reality, which allows users to feel like they are physically present in the virtual environment.

But what might an illusion of reality be useful for, or where lies the value of presence? Immersion and presence are certainly not appropriate or desirable for all learning situations. However, they can be useful in some cases, for instance where the learning context is physically inaccessible. One compelling use case for using immersive VR is learning a practical skill, which we can't practice in an authentic context. In this case, we'd want to provide a realistic simulation of the physical world that could support the transfer of learned skills into practice. To learn practical skills where learning by doing is useful, the promise of iVR lies in offering embodied experiences (as it allows free head and body movements) and hands-on, experiential learning. From an embodied cognition point of view (Varela, Thomson, & Rosch, 1991), cognition is not only in the brain, but also in sensorimotor activities. Piaget's (1964) work for instance, demonstrated that children's sensorimotor activities affect learning. Participation in immersive Virtual Environments allows users to experience vivid sensory information, which invokes bodily responses. Several VR studies (a.o. Bailey et al., 2017; Ekstrand et al., 2018; Parmar, 2017) indicated that sensorimotor activities in iVR can lead to positive learning outcomes. Through embodied experiences, learners construct contextualized understanding and gain knowledge and experiences that are embedded in practice.

Another question that arises is, how much immersion is enough to support positive learning outcomes? Desktop VR can be adequate for simulating behaviours, for creating a sense of presence and promoting learning. Research (a.o.

Barrett & Blackledge, 2012; Dede et al., 1997; Winn et al., 2001) has supported that desktop VR can be useful for training, as it is an interactive and engaging medium. However, several studies that compared non-immersive training methods, low-immersion VR (desktop VR) and high-immersion VR (iVR), have demonstrated that high immersion tends to demonstrate better performance and positive training outcomes. Examples of studies that compared (a) iVR with no immersion, and (b) iVR with desktop VR are provided in Table 4.1. While more research is needed before we can draw conclusions, iVR seems to be perceived as an enhancement to desktop VR, as evidenced by the available research.

TABLE 4.1 iVR vs. no VR and iVR versus desktop VR

Researchers	Date	Type of study and study purpose	Findings
		Immersive VR vs. No immersion	
Ekstrand et al.	2018	Randomized controlled study compared iVR training with paper-based training in neuro-anatomy. The study used a sample of n=64 medical students randomly assigned to the iVR group (n=31) using HTC Vive, or to the paper-based group (n=33).	The findings suggested that the VR group scored higher in the post-intervention test and the authors concluded that iVR was an effective learning tool which improved knowledge retention.
Pulijala et al.	2018	Randomized controlled study compared iVR training with training using PowerPoint slides. The study used a sample of n=91 novice surgery residents, randomly assigned to either an iVR group (Oculus Rift) (n=51) or a control group that received Power-Point training (n=40).	The VR group showed higher performance and significantly higher levels of confidence in performing surgical procedures than the control group.
Sankaranarayanan et al.	2018	Experimental study compared iVR versus in operating room fire prevention. After a week post-intervention test was administered to test knowledge, which was similar in both groups.	Another week after post-test, participants participated in a mock fire scenario. The findings showed that the iVR group performed significantly higher than the control group.

(Continued)

TABLE 4.1 (Cont.)

Researchers	Date	Type of study and study purpose	Findings
	**Immersive VR training vs low immersion, desktop VR**		
Bowman et al.	2010	Experimental study in which participants memorized procedures involving multiple steps in a virtual environment and then attempted to recall those procedures. The purpose of the study was to investigate the effect of immersion on performance by manipulating different levels of immersion.	The study demonstrated that higher immersion led to significantly more effective memorization and improved performance than lower levels of immersion.
Havranek et al.	2012	The study manipulated the degree of immersiveness of a video game environment by applying either an egocentric or an exocentric user perspective and examining whether the user felt spatially present.	The study found that high immersion and high spatial presence was achieved better from the user's egocentric perspective (i.e. first-person view) than if experienced it from an exocentric perspective (i.e. third-person view).
Stevens & Kincaid	2015	Experimental study, which examined whether higher presence in the virtual environment correlated with higher performance. The study used a sample of n=96 US Army male soldiers, who were placed in a flight simulator and were instructed to destroy synthetic enemy forces. Performance results were captured at the operator station and presence was measured right after the experience through a self-report measure by Witmer and Singer (1998).	The results of the study demonstrated that higher visual immersion correlated with higher presence and higher performance.
Bailey et al.	2017	In this experimental study, participants (n= 83) were randomly assigned to desktop VR, gesture-based VR, or voice-based VR.	The results of the study showed that iVR was effective for military based tasks as compared to desktop VR.

(*Continued*)

TABLE 4.1 (Cont.)

Researchers	Date	Type of study and study purpose	Findings
Parmar	2017	The study compared the effects of three levels of immersive embodied interactions on cognitive thinking, presence, usability, and satisfaction among users in the fields of science, technology, engineering, and mathematics (STEM) education. The three levels were: desktop VR (DVR), immersive VR (IVR), and immersive embodied VR (IEVR).	The results showed that iVR was effective in knowledge acquisition and retention and it enhanced user satisfaction. Users felt present and they were very engaged in the learning activities within the immersive VE.
Zhang et al.	2017	This experimental study examined the effectiveness of iVR for fire extinction training. The study used n= 60 randomly selected students, the first group was assigned to iVR, the second to desktop VR, and the third group used a textbook.	The findings of the study demonstrated the effectiveness of iVR in terms of fire extinction training as compared to desktop VR and to the non-VR training approach.

The (surmountable) challenges of iVR

iVR hasn't yet seen wide application aside from practical skills training. This may be due to the challenges associated with the technology. Some of the challenges of iVR technology are the following:

- *Cost*: due to its high cost, and the fact that high-end HMDs require a rather powerful computer. This challenge is diminishing however, as the price of even the high-end HMDs reduces over time (Moore's law), and as standalone, mobile HMDs have emerged, making iVR more accessible.
- *Cybersickness and discomfort*: HMDs and VR applications may sometimes cause cybersickness. The weight of HMDs can be uncomfortable for users over a longer period of time. Whilst this challenge hasn't been overcome yet, one expects that as the technology continues to evolve, HMDs will become lighter, and perhaps in the future even as light and small as normal glasses.
- *Learning curve*: another challenge that shouldn't be neglected is that few people are familiar with iVR technology. iVR use involves setting up the hardware and learning how to use it and how to navigate in the software application. This implies that unless already familiar with the technology,

coaching clients need to receive instructions and training prior to using VR in coaching sessions. However stand-alone devices like the Oculus Quest are showing that devices can be made to be set up easily and quickly.

- *The complexity of VR design*: designing VR content requires a high-level computer programming skill and graphics expertise. Technical capabilities also need to be coupled with the educational content. VR design requires transdisciplinary collaboration between technical and education specialists, in order to transfer the educational intention and appropriately depict the content in the VR environment. Technical specialists need to understand the education specialist's intention, and then to transfer, and to appropriately depict the verbal or written learning content in the VR environment.

Some of the challenges associated with immersive VR, such as cybersickness and the discomfort of wearing an HMD for a long time, remain. However, the breakthroughs in immersive Virtual Reality technology, particularly the advances in eye tracking, image resolution, the recent mobile, stand-alone version of VR that doesn't require a phone or a PC, and the diminishing challenges in terms of cost, bandwidth, and computer processing power, open up an expanded range of possible applications of this technology. The complexity of immersive VR content design is diminishing as well. Firstly, there is an increasing number of start-ups specializing in the design of VR educational and training contents. These companies get commissions to develop tailored training contents orscenarios (which is of course a costly option). Secondly, there are various asset repositories for downloading 3D models that allow non-developers to choose contents from a database to create their own scenario-based applications, thereby having maximum control of editing their virtual environment and with no programming needed. Thirdly, devices, such as 360° cameras, and eventually depth sensing cameras will allow us to capture User-Generated Content, which we can then view in VR, and thereby depend less on bespoke VR applications. All this makes VR content more accessible and relatively easy for users to create by themselves.

Applications of iVR within training and further education

Immersive Virtual Reality technology is applied to diverse fields, among which, design, engineering, mental health, gaming, education, and training. The idea behind it is generally simulation, whether it is simulation of real objects, products, designs, or life situations. Simulation provides a constructivist method for learning experientially. The learner actively experiments and learns by doing, just like he would be practicing and learning a skill in real life. The aim of immersive VR simulation is to replicate the real life setting accurately and to allow the user to construct knowledge, using as much as possible the same senses and body movements as he would use in reality. So far, immersive Virtual Reality has had successful use cases in training situations, where practicing a skill is required, but prevented by hazards (e.g. firefighting), high costs for physical arrangements (e.g. military operations and aerospace), and ethical constraints involved, when errors made in training can affect human lives (e.g. surgery). As the technology evolves and it becomes increasingly accessible, with reduced costs and complexity, improved capabilities and more accessible options for designing VR contents, it opens up an expanded range of applications, beyond practical training in elite sectors such as aerospace and the military. Examples of how iVR can be applied are:

- Scenario-based learning applications, where a sense of presence might be desirable to put oneself in other's shoes, or to develop empathy: e.g. the police force being trained in conflict de-escalation. iVR can also be used to ask the question 'what if?' and to encourage imagination, to expand thinking or to enable users to explore different possibilities.
- Educational applications to explore abstract concepts, e.g. physics, geometry, and biology (Bowman et al., 2010), where it would be desirable to physically interact with the concept. There is already some evidence to suggest its usefulness in conveying geometric concepts and memorizing abstract procedures.
- Situations where communication and support are needed as for instance:
  ○ Telepresence, to hold meetings remotely and potentially soon, for interacting with AI assistants by giving chatbots a holographic presence (a full body and an emotion expressing face).
  ○ Shadowing: through VR one could be present in the authentic context of the person they are supporting in real-time, if the learner attaches a 360° camera on her head or upper body.

The education field has started to embrace iVR technology as a way to make learning engaging and experiential, and to provide students non-symbolic experiences and learning by doing. Even though iVR hasn't been used to support coaching much at all until now, there are some signs that this could be changing. An article by Ebermann (2017) in Rauen's *Coaching-Magazin* described the multiple potential that iVR could have for coaching, such as offering safe environments and perspective changing. A recent Delphi study (Woods, 2018) with 15 expert coaches found that coaches were aware of iVR and its potential to supplement face-to-face coaching and to enhance coaching processes, and they predicted that there will be an increase in the use of iVR coaching in the future. Whether iVR will eventually be integrated in coaching practice or not, depends on the general adoption of this technology, which if it is high enough, it will bring down the cost for high-end HMDs. It's easy however, to imagine how iVR could be implemented in coaching contexts. The following sections provide five suggestions, based on the capabilities of specific iVR apps that are currently available on the market: telepresence, teleportation, simulation, shadowing, and creation/visualization by drawing or painting.

Immersive VR applications and coaching

Telepresence

Many immersive VR applications allow telepresence for remotely held sessions. They are typically used to socialize or to have a virtual work meeting, and they could easily be applied to run coaching sessions as well. These apps offer coaches the option to create a private room for themselves and their client – or clients in the case of team coaching – and to communicate via built-in audio chat. Typically, users can select and customize their avatar and enter the virtual environment from a first-person perspective. Coach and client sit together in the room like they would in a physical room. Some VR applications allow users who don't have HMDs to participate in the meeting on their computer, meaning that the coaching client, for instance, doesn't necessarily need an HMD.

In some applications (e.g. Anyworld), users can also enter different contexts (such as, an office, a beach, etc.) for the meeting to take place. Such a context could be used for instance, to explore an ideal situation, or simply to enjoy a pleasant, relaxing, or inspiring environment. In a private VR room (e.g. *Facebook Spaces VR* and *Bigscreen VR*), coach and client can also share resources, such as videos, images, PowerPoint presentations and 3D models that they view together. Perhaps soon, coaching clients will be able to interact with AI

FIGURE 4.2 Oculus Rooms

assistants, which will have a holographic presence, that is a full body and an emotion expressing face. The following VR applications offer the option to facilitate one-on-one, or group coaching sessions in a private VR room:

- *Bigscreen VR* allows to create a private room for up to four users, in a setting of their choice. Avatars are customizable. Users communicate with each other via built-in audio chat, and they can make presentations or share video resources. The application is offered for free and is compatible with the HMDs Oculus Rift, HTC Vive, and with mobile VR headsets.
- *Engage VR* allows to create and join meetings, but also to create and share contents. It can be used by coaches to hold coaching sessions, to make presentation, to write on a board. The app also allows to customize one's own avatar, by uploading a picture and letting the app choose a lifelike avatar that resembles the user closely. Another way in which coaches can use the app, is to create and publish coaching modules. Engage allows screensharing, it has full connectivity to the internet, allowing users to search resources and view them together in VR. It also allows to share 3D models and 360° videos.
- *LearnBrite* is an experiential learning authoring VR and AR tool. It allows to easily create scenarios in VR and AR, or on the desktop, mobile phone, or tablet. In LearnBrite users can select a space, among other, an office space, an exhibition hall, a boardroom and to customize it adding furniture and other items. Users are represented by customizable avatars who can teleport within the space. Meetings can be joined via audio and video conferencing, or through a VR headset. In

FIGURE 4.3 Bigscreen VR campfire environment

FIGURE 4.4 Bigscreen VR customizable avatar

addition, this application offers the option to create a human-like AI bot, which can be given a name, gestures, and a caption, for instance, a bot that is used to welcome participants in the meeting room, before the team coaching session begins. Users can use tools such as sticky notes, they can search content on the internet, share documents, videos, and presentations using a pointer just like in physical presentations.

- *Meetingroom.io* is a secure, cross platform application, allowing users to create and join meetings from their smartphone, desktop, or VR headsets. Up to 12 users with VR headsets can join the virtual meeting. Meetingroom.io could be very useful for team coaching, allowing to replicate the physical meeting and to collaborate using tools such as a whiteboard, sticky notes, presentation slides, and documents. Users are represented by a customizable avatar, above which, the name of the person is shown. When a person is speaking, the avatars of the rest of team turn towards the speaker. The application allows to see the other team members and to observe their body language, as they speak.

- *MeetinVR* is another iVR app that allows teams to participate in a virtual meeting and to collaborate. Among the tools this application offers are, mind maps and drawing tools. It also allows to upload and share media, such as PowerPoint presentations, audio and video files and 3D models, which can be discussed during the virtual meeting.
- *Rumii* is typically used for virtual collaboration of teams, also allows to create private rooms, to communicate via the built-in audio chat and screen sharing. Rumii is a multi-modal VR app, as it runs on HMDs, as well as on desktops and mobile devices (smartphones and tablets).
- *Roomful VR* allows users to create a personalized 3D room, from a smartphone, using photos, videos, and adding 3D decorations from the app's repository. The content can be shared in VR, AR HoloLens, desktop, smartphone, or tablet. Roomful offers a context for immersive virtual storytelling in a private room. It can be used for instance, by the client to describe the situation to the coach, or by the coach to share a story and to start dialogue with the client.
- *Rec Room, Steam VR Home, Oculus Rooms, VR chat,* and *AltSpaceVR* are further examples of VR applications that can be used to facilitate coaching sessions remotely, in a private room for the coach and client(s).

Teleportation: exploring new contexts/perspectives

iVR allows users to teleport and to explore different contexts. Coaching clients can be placed in, or teleport to different virtual environments to explore a desired or ideal for the client situation. Teleporting to a new environment can be used to activate clients' imagination, or to explore their emotions or reactions to a new place. How does the client feel walking around in the countryside? How does she feel flying over the skyscrapers of a busy city, or looking up a mountain from its foot? The following iVR applications offer possibilities to do so:

- *Anyworld*: users can teleport to pre-made polygonal environments, such as an office, a beach, or a country side and walk around there.
- *Google Earth VR*: the app allows users to teleport and walk around or fly over thousands of different real world locations in the world in near photographic quality. It allows to explore streets, to look down on the earth or on a city from above, and to look around 360°.
- *Google Expeditions VR*: offers 900 different curated expeditions for educational field trips, based on the 360° photography form Google Earth. It could potentially be applied to coaching, allowing clients to be placed in front of a waterfall, or to experience adventures such as a visit in outer space or swimming with sharks. Clients may teleport to the clouds, or they may put themselves in the shoes of different people as for instance, by experiencing a day in the life of a designer, a teacher, a manager, a surgeon, or an artist.

- *Google Earth VR Tour Creator*: can be used to capture and upload 360° videos and images, to create tours for clients, for instance around a modern busy city or the countryside.
- *Roomful VR*: allows users to create and customize a room, which they can then use for storytelling.
- *VR Mood Booster*: is a simple VR app used for relaxation, meditation, and mood boosting. The app places the user in a calm environment that changes colours, combined with compatible sounds. It could be used in combination with coaching, for instance in between coaching sessions, for stress management and a calm place for clients to reflect and to collect their thoughts.
- *Wander VR*: this is the Mobile VR version of Google Street View but unlike Street View of Google Earth VR, Wander allows users to do this with other users who can be located anywhere in the real world with a good enough internet connection.
- Through *360° cameras*, one could also easily capture real-life situations and contexts to be viewed in VR (as for instance, in the app Engage VR).

Simulations

Simulations can be used for clients to play out different roles, or to test potential scenarios and situations (e.g. being put in a stressful situation), as role-play activities. Through 360° and live streaming, one could capture real-life situations and contexts, such as for instance, a calm landscape or an office scenario, where coachees can observe two people have a quarrel, or another difficult situation, which could then be used to view and discuss them in VR with the client. As an alternative to UGC, some VR apps offer a selection of different contexts that can be used for coaching purposes:

FIGURE 4.5 Microsoft Maquette – 3D environment for doing user experience mock-ups

FIGURE 4.6 Oculus Home – example of environment that can be created and set as home space

- *Rec Room*: allows users to create any 3D object and context in which, they can have their dialogue.
- *SonoVR*: is a VR prototype application of different interventions that can be used in coaching and mental health to support behaviour change.
- *Mindshow*: allows users to create different characters and virtually act in their bodies for role play and storytelling.
- *Ovation*: this VR app is used to simulate and practice public speaking. It could be used in a coaching context, for clients to practice their speaking and presentation skills and to share and discuss their progress with their coach in a safe, but realistic environment.

FIGURE 4.7 VR Mood Booster (Credits: Dana-Maria Faneker, founder of the VR Mood Booster)

Shadowing

Aside from the basic coaching dialogue, VR technology can also be useful in situations where support is needed to transfer intended behaviours or actions into practice, for instance it can be used for shadowing. In VR, the coach can 'be' at the authentic context of the client, observe and support them in real-time (via live streaming), as the client uses a 360° camera to capture a situation in her daily or work life. The client may either use a wearable 360° camera, allowing the client to observe the situation where the action takes place from the client's perspective, or a camera could be placed in the room to allow the coach to observe both, the client and the situation, e.g. the interaction with others.

Drawing, painting, and whiteboard VR tools

Some VR applications include tools to create 3D objects. *Rec Room* for instance, offers a powerful 'creator pen' tool to create any 3D object, and even the logic to control and create interactivity.

Rather than drawing on a piece of paper, on a board, or a screen, VR enables users to draw or to paint in a three-dimensional space, and all around ourselves. Among the VR apps that allow 3D drawing/whiteboarding/painting are: *AltSpaceVR*, *Facebook Spaces VR*, *Rumii*, *TiltBrush*, *SculptrVR*, and *Bigscreen VR*.

TiltBrush is a VR painting application through which users can create and explore brushstrokes with different colours, textures, and volumes in room-scale, using the space in any direction. Users can walk around their own painting, look at it from different perspectives, minimize, enlarge, rotate, or move it and save it. The painting can also be animated and combined with music. Moreover, paintings

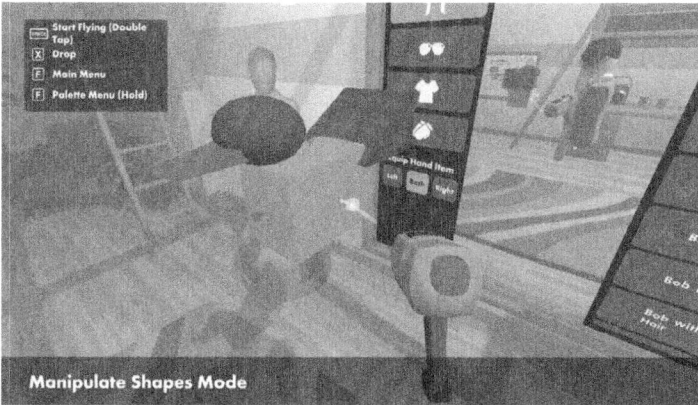

FIGURE 4.8 3D painting in Rec Room

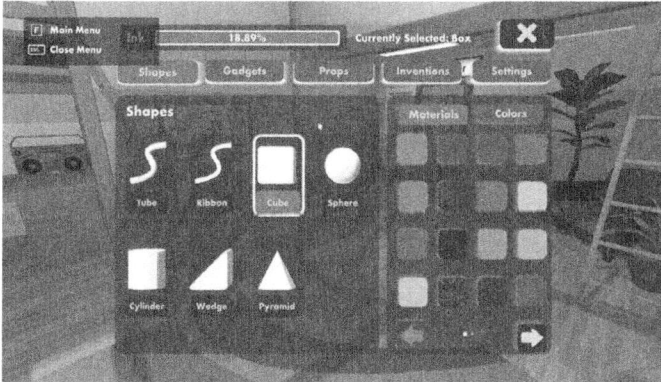

FIGURE 4.9 Rec Room creator pen palette

FIGURE 4.10 3D sketching in Bigscreen VR

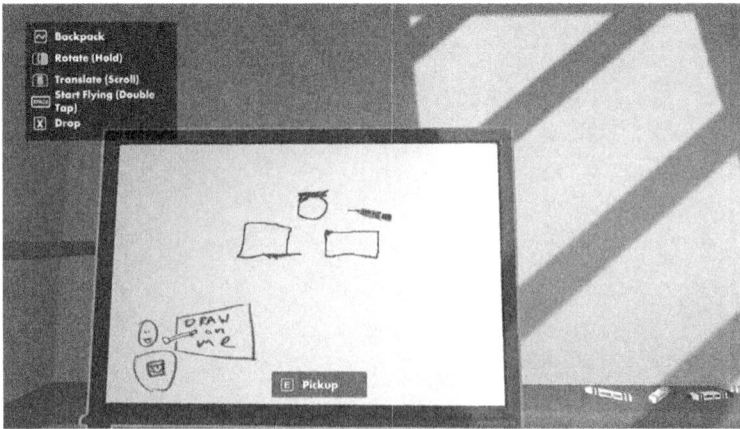

FIGURE 4.11 Whiteboard in Rec Room

created in TiltBrush can be exported and saved either privately or publicly on *Google Poly*, a dedicated platform for downloading and accessing 3D content. Users can also capture snapshots of their creations and render 360° videos. The case study in Box 4.1 illustrates how TiltBrush can be integrated in the coaching process.

BOX 4.1 CASE EXAMPLE: COACHING WITH TILTBRUSH

The art-analogue coaching approach combines traditional coaching tools with artistic processes, such as performances, installations, sound experiments, music, painting, or lyrics, to support individuals, teams and organizations within their individual change processes. Coachees learn through artistic practices to use their own resources to develop new perspectives and strategies for personal and professional challenges. The art-analogue coaching process can be described in three simple phases:

- *Phase 1*: Clarification of the coaching problem.
- *Phase 2*: Decentralization, which involves using an analogue or digital medium to intentionally temporarily move away from the problem. The coach focuses on the client's aesthetic perception within the artistic process and asks reflective questions about the client's perceived qualities and surfaces of the physical/digital objects, sounds, movements and other noticeable emergences, as well as about the client's emotional reactions to the object.
- *Phase 3:* Resource activation: the coachee is asked, which experiences and action strategies could be used to solve the coaching problem.

Susanne was a Master's student of art-analogue coaching at the Medical School, Hamburg. Aside from physical materials, she integrated TiltBrush in the coaching process with one of her coachees. Based on her experience with TiltBrush, the coachee is confronted with an open, artistic process, which offers new perspectives and perceptions. Even though perceived aesthetic experiences in VR may initially seem to be limited compared to analogue haptic materials (e.g. one can't touch or smell virtual objects), VR experiences allow new and different experiences, such as walking through shapes and around an object, visualizing movements, observing an object in full scale, leading to new aesthetic perspectives.

FIGURE 4.12 Material and dimension studies in TiltBrush

The problem

A freelancer wanted to understand how to deal with different challenges in the daily working routine, and to avoid getting lost in micromanagement activities. The goal was to increase mindfulness and to change from micromanagement to a bird's-eye view perspective.

The process

Following familiarization with TiltBrush, the coach asked the coachee to try out different movements that would represent for her how the solved problem would 'feel' like. The coachee used a brush in TiltBrush and made several circular hand movements.

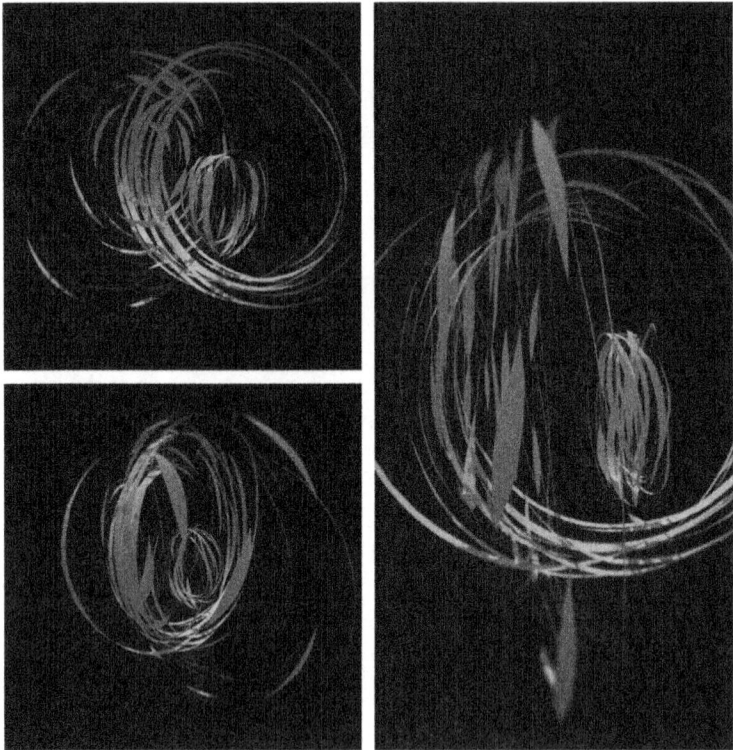

FIGURE 4.13   The coachee's creations in TiltBrush (Credits to Susanne Dold)

Soon, the coachee stopped concentrating on the movements and started to focus more on the actual drawing that was unfolding, two merging circles, a large and a small. The coach asked a series of questions to encourage the coachee's reflection on the created drawing. Through this reflection process the coachee reached the conclusion that 'daily routine means a constant flow between the two conditions'. When getting stuck in one condition, the coachee understood that setting this 'in motion' might help to regain control, be creative, and save time. While looking at two objectives in the 3D virtual room, the two conditions merged together. The coachee became aware that both conditions have to be in balance and that in doing so, motion is important. Another key insight for the coachee was that mindfulness of the two conditions was important for maintaining an overview.

Mapping VR applications

VR applications can have one specific function or several functions, as described earlier, e.g. painting, telecommunication in a private room, teleporting, object creation, etc. (see Table 4.3 for an overview). Hardware, specifically 360° cameras are also included in Table 4.3, as they allow coaches and clients to capture User-Generated Content, for instance, to create scenarios from everyday life or they could be used for shadowing.

BOX 4.2 CASE EXAMPLE: USING A 360° CAMERA FOR SHADOWING

Marc is a new manager, with very little experience in managing people. When he gets stressed, he tends to get impatient with his team and to carry out the task himself, rather than to delegate tasks to the team, or to be demanding and short with them. Marc is increasingly feeling overwhelmed and stressed.

In their previous coaching session, Marc agreed with his coach to try to listen to the team, to show trust, and not to over-control the situation. What Marc intends to change, is to try and work with his team, to reflect with them on what went wrong and why, and how could they improve things next time.

Marc and his coach have agreed that it would be helpful if the coach accompanies Marc, as he is trying to change. Marc uses a small 360° camera to capture the meeting with his team, which the coach can observe real-time via web-streaming.

After the meeting, coach and client have a coaching session in the VR app Engage, where they can view again the 360° video, reconstruct the conversation with Marc's team, reflect and discuss how the meeting with the team went.

Some of the iVR apps (such as TiltBrush, VR Mood Booster) are location-dependent, as they only support one user. This means that the client is placed in the VR environment, while the coach is a spectator of the client's environment from the desktop that the HMD is connected to. The implication is that coach and client are not co-present in the virtual environment and can only interact with one another if they are co-located.

Example: The client is painting in TiltBrush. The coach follows the client's brushstrokes and movement by looking at the client's activity on the desktop and guides the client with prompts and reflexive questions.

Other apps (such as AltspaceVR, Meetinroom.io, MeetinVR, Engage, Rec Room, Facebook Spaces VR) are cross-dimensional, and so they can be accessed

TABLE 4.2 iVR applications and types

App/hardware	Telepresence (in private space)	Share resources	Create/download/teleport and explore VEs	3D object creation/VE creation	3D painting/drawing/whiteboard	Suitable for shadowing	Simulations (scenarios)
Anyworld	✓	✓	✓	✓		✓	✓
AltspaceVR	✓	✓			✓		
Bigscreen VR	✓	✓			✓		
Engage	✓	✓		✓	✓	✓	
Facebook Spaces	✓	✓	✓				
Google Earth VR			✓				
Google Earth Tour Creator			✓				
Google Expeditions VR			✓				
LearnBrite	✓	✓	✓	✓	✓		✓
Meetingroom.io	✓	✓	✓		✓		
MeetinVR	✓	✓	✓		✓		
Mindshow	✓						✓
Ovation							✓
Rec Room	✓	✓		✓	✓		✓
Roomful	✓	✓	✓	✓	✓		
Rumii	✓			✓			
SonoVR	✓			✓	✓		✓
TiltBrush			✓	✓	✓		
Virtway Events	✓		✓				
VR Chat	✓		✓	✓	✓		
VR Mood Booster			✓				
Wander VR						✓	
360 camera UGC							

and used in VR through HMDs, but also from a desktop or a mobile device, meaning that coach and client are not location dependent and they can interact with one another from different places. Such apps are multi-user platforms.

> *Example:* The client creates a virtual environment with 3D objects in Rec Room. The coach accesses the Rec Room app and interacts with the client via the Rec Room voice-chat from her desktop.

TABLE 4.3 Forms of coaching in iVR – face-to-face and remote coaching options

	Location		Access		Users	
App	*Location-dependent*	*Location independent*	*Cross-dimensional*	*VR only*	*Single user*	*Multi-user*
Anyworld		✓		✓		✓
AltspaceVR		✓	✓			✓
Bigscreen VR		✓		✓		✓
Engage	✓			✓		✓
Facebook Spaces		✓		✓		✓
Google Earth VR	✓			✓	✓	
Google Earth Tour Creator	✓			✓	✓	
Google Expeditions VR	✓			✓	✓	
LearnBrite		✓	✓			✓
Meetinroom.io		✓	✓			✓
meetinVR		✓	✓			✓
Mindshow					✓	
Ovation	✓			✓	✓	
Rec Room		✓	✓			✓
Roomful		✓	✓			✓
Rumii		✓	✓			✓
SonoVR	✓			✓	✓	
TiltBrush	✓			✓	✓	
Virtway Events		✓	✓			
VR Chat		✓				
VR Mood Booster	✓			✓	✓	
Wander VR	✓			✓		✓

The VR coaching experience

Immersive VR technology has the potential to take remote coaching experiences to a new level, as it allows highly interactive and embodied actions. Entering a virtual environment, looking around 360° degrees and vertically up and down, walking towards an object, all around it and inside it (e.g. going inside a ship or a building) offer completely different experiences from looking at images on a flat computer screen. The immersive Virtual Reality experience can be intense, engaging, interactive, and it can feel realistic. One can have an exciting roller-coaster experience, or a walk in the forest on a calm, sunny morning. Virtual environments with objects and people in full scale enable spatial experiences comparable to those in real life. They create a sense of existing in the environment. These advantages apply to one-on-one coaching as well as to team coaching, as VR enables teams to interact, brainstorm together, and collaborate with one another. Interacting with objects (e.g. moving a chair, or throwing a ball), getting underneath a table, standing on a theatre stage, or holding virtual hands and dancing with an avatar offer an active, learning by doing approach to acquiring new skills and behaviours. Through such embodied, kinaesthetic experiences coaching clients actively construct their knowledge and experiment with their environment. Rather than relying only on words, coaching clients have the chance to test potential solutions to a problem and to let themselves free to create in a safe, but realistic environment. The rich and powerful VR experiences can be useful for coaching, allowing clients to teleport to different places and contexts to stimulate their imagination, to practice skills (e.g. presentation skills), or to simulate different situations (e.g. an interpersonal conflict) and reflect on different scenarios.

TABLE 4.4 The features and targeted effects of iVR in coaching

Feature	Targeted effect
Natural head and body movements	✓ Kinaesthetic experience ✓ Increased sense of presence
Experiencing full scale objects and environments	✓ Realistic experience ✓ Sense of presence
Changing the scale of objects, i.e. enlarging or minimizing objects	✓ Different points of view relative to the object (e.g. user is big as compared to the minimized object) ✓ Imagine new perspectives
Physical interaction with a virtual environment	✓ Interactivity ✓ Engagement and active learning
Teleporting to different environments	✓ Being placed in an inspiring context (e.g. a beautiful island) and coaching in places, where traditional coaching couldn't typically take place (e.g. the top of a mountain) ✓ Stimulating imagination ('what would it be like if ...')

The ongoing technological advancements, the emergence of consumer VR, and the reducing selling price of HMD devices could drive increased application of iVR technology in coaching. Even though the challenges of iVR are diminishing, it remains to be seen whether the time and cost needed to create truly useful VR apps can be balanced by the benefits for the coaching process.

Currently, tailored VR content is very limited. In the years to come however, as coaches begin to use this technology more, this could change. The already existing desktop-based VR coaching software could evolve to apply to immersive VR technology, if the technology attracts enough interest by coaches.

Creating scenarios in VR for coaching could be done without costly and time-consuming programming of VR apps, by creating or downloading a room or context (e.g. an office, a beach etc.) from an asset repository, and downloading different AI agents (e.g. angry, bossy, compliant). We are already seeing some VR apps (e.g. Engage, MeetinVR, and meetingroom.io), which are offering some of these capabilities. Humanoid-like avatars with AI elements (e.g. LearnBrite) could become more prominent in coaching in the future, opening up possibilities for delivering AI-assisted coaching on simple coaching issues.

The client can be placed in, and be part of the scenarios that are created in VR, and then reflect upon them with the coach. The use of 360° cameras could also be usefully applied to coaching for shadowing or for reflecting on real life situations. Capturing content for VR experiences could eventually become as easy and natural as it is to make high quality video recording on one's phone today. Some VR apps (e.g. Engage) allow the coach to create coaching modules that can be offered for self-coaching. There are many VR apps that are allowing to replicate the physical meeting and allow teams to collaborate, using Post-its, sharing content in the form of video or documents, whiteboarding, and sketching.

What we are also beginning to see is VR technology to enable users (coach and clients) to meet in VR for their coaching session, and whilst in VR, to switch between various VR apps to carry out a task, such as, to view a 3D model, to create a mind map, or a painting, and to go on stage to practice a speech. Rather than looking for the optimal VR app for coaching, coach and client can use their meeting in VR to search for a VR tool appropriate for a given task without leaving the meeting. Using this 'ecosystem' of VR tools, the coaching interaction gains flexibility and seamlessness. Technology is there for the coach and client to exploit, without having to interrupt the coaching session.

Augmented Reality

The state of the art and applications of AR

In contrast to Virtual Reality, which isolates the user from the physical environment to enable immersion, Augmented Reality superimposes 3D models onto the physical world. Like Virtual Reality technology, Augmented Reality is also not completely new. In a way, Sutherland's Sensorama (1968) was an

Augmented Reality technology, as it didn't completely isolate the user from the physical environment, but users could still see their surroundings. In the 1990s, NASA used Augmented Reality technology to navigate their spacecraft. A little later, the automobile industry used AR to build cars.

It wasn't until 2016 that AR technology's breakthrough, the Microsoft Holo-Lens became available to consumers. The HoloLens is the first commercial device featuring mobile, head mounted spatial awareness (i.e. the device makes a 3D model of its surroundings in near real time). The HoloLens took advantage of a form of computer vision technology called depth sensing that initially debut on Microsoft's Xbox gaming console which had an accessory called, Kinect. The Kinect could create a 3D depth model of what it saw through its two cameras and infrared time of flight sensors. The HoloLens used this technology (which in the meantime has been replaced by feature point recognition technology) to understand where in space the headset was, therefore enabling the stable and persistent placement of virtual objects in the physical space, as well as the tracking of the headset in space.

AR is being applied to the areas of education and training, the automobile industry, health care, manufacturing, and marketing, among other industries. It supports collaborative work for teams to view together and discuss 3D models, it allows to visualize solutions to facilitate and reduce the costs for design and production, and it supports interactive learning and the understanding of concepts, by visually mapping them and allowing the learner to experiment with them. The HoloLens still comes at a significant cost, so far preventing or making unlikely its application by individual professionals, or small practices, like coaching practices.

Beyond the HoloLens on the other hand, AR is becoming more accessible through mobile devices, which nowadays include all necessary components for AR, such as accelerometers, improved cameras, and GPS. Mobile AR was initiated by Google's Tango technology, which used multiple cameras and sensors to enable phone-based AR, placing and anchoring virtual objects in the physical space to create the illusion that they are in one's physical environment. Following the Tango project, the continued breakthroughs in AR have been based on monoscopic phone cameras with both Apple and Google developing algorithms that can determine what the camera is looking at and where it is in 3D space. These algorithms have been bundled into software development kits (ARCore and ARKit) and are improving rapidly. Smartphones have started to have the ability to detect the object we are looking at, as they include positional tracking (they integrate accelerators and sensors) and plane recognition (plane detection with depth cameras was a technology that allowed accurate positioning of virtual objects in the real world). They can now place and anchor virtual objects in the real world in a convincing way. The most recent breakthroughs have been in the use of the Cloud infrastructure to enable multi-user AR experiences, where multiple users can see the same virtual objects in the same places in the physical world. Mobile AR will be significant in broadening the applications of AR and making this technology accessible.

Potential uses of AR in coaching

If AR (HMD or mobile-based) becomes more accessible in terms of its costs and performance, how might coaches put this technology in use? Below are some possible scenarios:

Holographic telepresence

What we are missing in VR is the capability of the technology to see the other person (not the avatar of the person). This is a barrier that AR technology can overcome with holographic telepresence. Projecting real-time 3D images of individuals would certainly revolutionize remote communication. It would also have significant implications for coaching practice, as it would mean that coach and client can have a remote session and see not just each other's face, but also the whole person in 3D and each other's context, shake hands, and have the sense that they are meeting physically.

Communicating with people by placing holograms of the other person in one's own environment is an exciting possibility. Whilst the technology is not quite fully developed yet, all the necessary technological features to allow holo-portation exist today, and so it's something we'll be seeing soon. The Azure Kinect AI camera allows body tracking and capture of accurate 3D models of people that can be rendered in a virtual space. Using AR or VR HMDs, the Azure Kinect will be the key feature to enable remote communication by seeing a true-scale holographic representation of a person. This technology will allow to coach remotely, as if coach and client were meeting physically. In the future, coach and client could be skyping with holoportation.

Visualization for problem-solving: drawing, painting, creating, and mind-mapping

Visual tools, such as drawing/painting, and constellations are used to support clients' thought processes and to complement verbal expression. Such tools exist as traditional media, such as drawing on paper or creating a physical constellation to represent inter-personal relationships, and as digital media, as discussed so far in this book. Beyond the contribution of VR applications, which allow representations in 3D, embodied actions, and high interactivity and thus, potentially high engagement, AR applications for drawing/painting, or for creating 3D objects and placing them around could be interesting for coaching, as they allow a combination and merging of clients' virtual and physical environments. Unless coach and client are interacting via distance using holoportation, the use case for these tools is to support face-to-face coaching or to be used in between coaching sessions. Examples include the following:

- *HoloBrush*: a 3D painting app for the HoloLens. Similar to VR painting apps, one can use different colour brushes to paint in 3D. The difference to VR is that, the user can view their painting while also being able to see their physical environment.
- *HoloBlocks*: this app allows creations using cube, cylinder, wedge, bridge, and dome 3D shapes. HoloBlocks could be used for constellation work as part of coaching, to create symbolic objects relevant to the client's issue.
- *Loci*: a mind-mapping application for the HoloLens. It allows users to create interactive mind maps, by placing nodes with images and descriptions for each node and linking them together for analysis. It can be used for visualization to support problem analysis and problem solving.

How applicable is AR for coaching?

The use of AR could enhance coaching, as other media can – from traditional media, e.g. pen and paper, to computer-based applications, including constellation tools or whiteboarding software, to VR apps. The advantage of AR is that clients can still see their coach in a face-to-face session and their environment, whilst at the same time focusing on a vivid representation of a virtual 3D object or person. The interactivity with the virtual environment is similar to that in immersive VR technology, but AR could be more intuitive and comfortable to use. HoloLens users make specific hand gestures to navigate, instead of holding hand controllers. The HoloLens HMD doesn't isolate users from their physical environment, which also reduces the risk of physical injury. AR is currently more applicable to face-to-face coaching, as options for remote telepresence in AR are not fully developed. In the future, AR could disrupt coaching, as holographic telepresence could even potentially replace desktop-based video conferencing and it could possibly also decrease traditional-face-to-face coaching. In coaching sessions, where coach and client meet virtually and see each other's hologram, the 3D representation of the person in full scale in their own context as if they were sitting together in the same room, wouldn't differ much at all from traditional face-to-face coaching sessions. Holoportation is not only possible with AR technology, offering telepresence without isolating one from their physical environment, but also with VR technology, whereby holographic telepresence coaching sessions could be combined with enhancing VR media, such as immersive scenarios.

Coaching and Artificial Intelligence

The exponentially maturing AI

The story of Artificial Intelligence (AI) goes several decades back. Since Turing's test in the 1950s, which put forward the idea that machines can think, and the research that was conducted in the 50s, 60s, and 70s (a.o. Allen Newell, 1956;

Herbert Simon, 1957; John McCarthy, 1959; Marvin Minsky, 1967, 1970), developments over the last 30 years have been exponential. These developments have been driven by the gains in computer processing power, as well as the access to large amounts of data, allowing to feed machines and getting them to learn.

Today's focus in the area of AI is very much on Machine Learning, due to the major breakthrough in the development and subsequent commercialization of Graphical Processing Units (GPUs) in the late 1990s. GPUs were originally intended and developed for gaming and industrial 3D applications, but it turned out that they were good at running large parallel calculations, the kind needed to train neural networks. The chess and Go game projects are obvious examples of how rapidly AI has advanced. In 1997, IBM's ground-breaking Deep Blue beat the world champion in chess, Garry Kasparov. In the last few years, the rate of development has been impressive. In 2016, using Machine Learning, Google Deep Mind's program AlphaGo beat the professional Go player, Lee Sedol, whilst the subsequent version, AlphaGo Master beat several professional Go players, among which, Ke Jie in 2017, who was the Go world champion at that time. In 2017, the self-taught AlphaGo Zero (it played against itself for a few hours) was much more powerful than any of its previous versions, beating not only human players after a couple of hours, but also machines (Stockfish) after a few more hours of reinforcement learning.

Clearly, the development of the World Wide Web has enabled to copy and distribute enormous amounts of data, initially only text and then audio, but nowadays also high-resolution video and even 3D scanned data. With the power of the Cloud and the development of large infrastructure providers, like Microsoft and Amazon, there is a huge amount of processing power available to train algorithms. Comparing modern devices with the computers of the past, there is a wide difference to computational power. This access to super computing power and to freely available big data has resulted in impressive developments in AI and Machine Learning (ML). Good examples are Google's Translate app, which can translate text on the fly via a phone's camera, or Google's ability to hear audio and turn it accurately into text with the voice search capability. Google even has algorithms that can convincingly create human-like voices, or even translate spoken audio into foreign languages in the speakers' own voice. With computing power only increasing and the volume of data made available, the now exploding Machine Learning and the resulting algorithms will become ubiquitous. Machines are clearly capable of approximating human reasoning to make decisions that could even supersede human cognition. Taking autonomous driving, sensors in the car can identify the pedestrian in the path of the car, then AI determines that it's in a collision course with the car and it makes the decision to put the brakes on. Unlike the human driver, the AI is always sober, free from emotions, doesn't get distracted, doesn't have 'bad days', thereby potentially less prone to error than humans. The advantages in terms of efficiency and neutrality, making decisions free from emotions and other distractions, can be significant.

Conversational interfaces

Recent developments in HCI include conversational interfaces (chatbots and voice assistants), as well as gesture recognition and eye tracking technologies. The first chatbot (ELIZA), using Natural Language Processing was created way back in the 1960s by Joseph Weizenbaum. Since then, conversational interfaces have significantly improved due to the advances in Natural Language Processing (speech recognition, allowing to understand human language), the HCI evolution and computational processing power (processing large amounts of information), enabling us to use chatbots and voice assistants in daily personal and professional life to support us in various tasks, and they are starting to have practical value for us. Today, we interact with intelligent devices to obtain information (e.g. about the weather, the news, facts), to have a very simple conversation, to get support in daily tasks (e.g. reminders, appointments), to ask for instructions. Conversational interfaces today are limited to such simple tasks, yet their functionality is growing.

The state of the art in AI-assisted coaching

Over the last few years, we can observe the development of numerous AI-powered coaching chatbots and voice-enabled conversational assistants (see Table 4.5). Many of these AI coaching apps perform quite simple tasks, such as suggesting relevant online resources, based on the information they gather about the coachee's type of issue, or providing feedback or tips on specific topics. Some of the available chatbots use algorithms that allow coaching interactions based on methods or coaching models, such as NLP, GROW (Pocket-Confidant), or CBT (Woebot, Wysa) to encourage coachees' reflection. These chatbots are not capable of unrestrained conversations yet and they can't read emotions and body language. They also can't respond with emotion. However, they do have the potential to provide support in certain aspects of the coaching process and in this sense, they can complement the work of the human coach and save time. For instance, they may support coaching clients with questions to help them reflect on their strengths, their course of action and decision-making processes. We can expect that their utility will become increasingly robust in the future as they continue to be trained with hundreds of coaching conversations, and AI-powered chatbots could eventually, replace some of the specialized apps.

TABLE 4.5 AI-powered tools

AI-powered tools	Description
BRiN	BRiN is an AI-powered chatbot programmed with thousands of business conversations. Users can chat to it about a business problem they are facing, and it links them with relevant video resources.
Butterfly	A management coaching chatbot from employee feedback. Based on anonymous survey feedback received from team members, the AI chatbot, Alex, helps managers improve their managerial skills in 50 workplace topics and it provides real-time visual team feedback. It then suggests relevant video resources to support managers further.
Coach Amanda	Coachees can chat with management coaching chatbot, Amanda, about employee problems and leadership issues. Amanda provides tips on employee problems and suggests ways to increase employee engagement and also provides micro-learning lessons on leadership topics such as delegation and feedback. It includes a Big Five personality assessment, which allows to provide suggestions based on personality type.
Charlie	Charlie is a chatbot available on Facebook Messenger by invitation only, that supports coachees' reflection on their values and strengths, and it helps them discover areas to improve. It provides assistance in issues such as, work-life balance, career transition, leadership, and helps to create new habits.
CoachBot	CoachBot, developed by Saberr, supports teams to improve their work processes. The first sessions with chatbot aim to identify common goals. Along the process, team members are regularly asked by chatbot to reflect on their progress. The chatbot gathers members' out comes and shares them with the whole team.
IBM® Watson™ Career Coach	Coachees are initially introduced to chatbot Myca, which chats with them about career questions such as 'Which jobs am I a good fit for?'. Watson Career Coach shows what might other people in a career role do next, it analyses coachees' preferences and job history and suggests matching roles for them and helps them create a career plan.
iThrive	The iThrive chatbot captures coachees' progress towards their goal and prompts other iThrive users to provide encouragement and support. iThrive focuses on changing habits and supporting coachees in achieving positive behaviour change.
LeaderAmp	LeaderAmp offers AI-based coaching prompts based on coachees' goals, within 18 areas of leader potential and performance. LeaderAmp includes a chatbot interface, Instant Coach, to support coachees in improving their persuasion skills. In addition, it includes a voice-to-text journal, in-app chat option with a coach, and the possibility for stakeholders who complete a 360° feedback to receive AI-powered suggestions via text about how they can support the coachee.

(Continued)

TABLE 4.5 (Cont.)

AI-powered tools	Description
Orai	Orai is an AI-powered e-learning app, which is offered as part of the company Duarte's coaching program in combination with digital individual coaching. Orai registers the speed of the speaker's speech, the filling words (e.g. uhm), and the clarity of speech, and it offers feedback and tips, based on data obtained from other presentations. It also offers opportunities for audio-recording and playback of the presentation, as well as transcription.
PocketConfidant	The PocketConfidant chatbot supports users as it helps them reflect on leadership and education-related issues. It can also be customized however, for other topics.
Tess	Tess is an AI-powered mental health chatbot supporting users' emotional wellness and coping strategies.
Woebot	Woebot is an AI-powered mental health chatbot using methods from Cognitive Behavioural Therapy to help users reflect on their mood and emotions. It suggests relevant content, in the form of stories or exercises.
Wysa	An AI-powered mental health chatbot with a cognitive-behavioural focus. Wysa can be used to chat about stress, anxiety, and other issues. It aims to support reflection and allows mind-fulness activities. Wysa offers the option to chat anonymously with a human coach.

BOX 4.3 CASE EXAMPLE: AI-ASSISTED MOBILE COACHING PLATFORM, LEADERAMP HELPS COSUMNES (CALIF.) FIRE CHIEF FIND TIME AND BUDGET TO IMPROVE HIS LEADER-SHIP SKILLS

Industry: public sector

Background

With an operating budget of $36 million, Cosumnes Fire Department, located in Northern California south of Sacramento, is one of the largest community services districts in the country. Employing nearly 2,000 firefighters and other staff, Cosumnes Fire works to fire and emergency medical services in the communities of Elk Grove and Galt.

Challenge

Cosumnes Fire Chief Michael McLaughlin wanted to develop his leadership skills to manage a large department more effectively, but with limited funds available for individual leader coaching and an always-on-call, time-demanding role, he needed a solution that was economical and that could work around his busy schedule.

Solution

McLaughlin was the first person in his organization to undergo LeaderAmp's leader coaching program. After a short digital assessment, McLaughlin chose to receive AI-powered eCoaching twice a week in time management and charisma, in addition to weekly 30-minute live video coaching sessions. In the next three months, McLaughlin wrote 31 journal entries and sent five private questions to his coach, while his coach nudged, supported, or sent kudos to McLaughlin 42 times and answered all five of his private questions. To help McLaughlin improve his time management skills, his coach evaluated recordings of him giving speeches, sent him videos and other resources demonstrating charisma role models, and sent him evidence-supported suggestions for improving his time management and charisma. LeaderAmp's AI-assisted Clone Coaching software offered McLaughlin tailored assignments to practice in his day-to-day duties, prompted him to make journal entries, and provided him checklists of behaviours to follow and report back on. The app also tracked how engaged McLaughlin's stakeholders – friends and colleagues who agree to support the LeaderAmp participant in their coaching program – were, ensuring that he received the feedback and encouragement he needed to complete the program.

Results

Mix of video one-on-one leader coaching sessions and AI-powered Clone Coaching allowed McLaughlin to work on his leadership skills whenever and wherever he found the time. McLaughlin's time management score improved by two levels, from proficient to master, in one quarter, while his Charisma 360 score increased from proficient to expert in the same period of time McLaughlin is now expanding the LeaderAmp program throughout his district for use by leaders at all levels.

AI could also certainly free coaches from having to write notes during their sessions. Natural Language Speech Recognition has enabled the development of AI-powered voice transcription apps (e.g. Otter, Tetra, Nuance Transcription Engine, and Zoom), which can be used to transcribe voice call conversations, thereby saving time and allowing the coach to focus on the conversation. Whilst they are currently somewhat limited, their quality will continue to improve over time.

Moreover, AI will probably be used for further simple tasks within the coaching process in the future, such as scheduling appointments, matching, providing simple questionnaires, assisting particularly with less complex coaching issues, providing analytics, and detecting patterns.

The currently available coaching chatbots are not, or at least not yet, an alternative to coaching sessions with a human coach, as their content has limited scope and their functionality is currently perhaps too limited to be considered serious coaching offers. Nevertheless, coaching chatbots can provide certain clear advantages:

- They offer tireless coaching support whenever needed and without having to schedule a session.
- They are neutral, non-judgemental partners that we can open up to.
- They could efficiently analyse client data based on their responses, and identify patterns of behaviour, which could help clients set an action plan for achieving their goals.
- They offer a written record of the coaching session that coach and client can refer to.

As AI matures, and as machines are fed more data, the capability of these chatbots will certainly evolve. Coaching chatbots in the future will have learned from thousands of coaching conversations to ask more intelligent questions, covering a wider range of topics, and they'll become better at detecting human emotions from analysis of the words used and even from coachees' tone of voice, and they might also learn to offer empathetic responses to some extent. Lifelike avatars in VR environments (even though many dislike the uncanny valley or they are confused by the high realism) or as holograms could give AI agents a human-like appearance. Even if the appearance is not highly realistic, in any case putting a face to the machine we are speaking to, could be helpful for us to perceive the AI coach as our personal coach, and not too much of a stranger or a heartless machine. Coaching chatbots that replicate the coaching relationship and become capable of offering truly valuable coaching may be an uncanny fantasy at the moment, but is it a completely impossible one to turn into reality in the future?

The future of an AI-powered coaching

As AI advances, the possibility that AI could become super intelligent is becoming a serious concern for many, including Stephen Hawking, Bill Gates, and Elon Musk, whilst some are still doubtful that AI can ever supersede humans and take over control. Where there is a little less doubt, is about the possibility of job replacements by AI. Frey and Osborne's study in 2013 predicted that 47% of jobs will be lost. Already many jobs are being replaced, because machines are more efficient, make fewer errors, and their performance is more reliable than that of humans. They perform simple, repetitive tasks, but they also perform some more complex tasks and automate processes. This means that more room is made for humans to perform higher-level tasks, tasks that require emotional intelligence and insight, and that new jobs can be created. Along with these benefits, it also creates new and significant challenges, anxiety and job insecurity, as well as the need to upskill.

As AI continues to perform increasingly complex human tasks, the role of humans will become increasingly to supervise AI, to ensure smooth performance, and to control for errors, and to use AI for enhancing humans' intelligence and skills and achieving better results. More specifically:

* *Firstly*, even if AI performs a task, humans still need to train in case of error (edge cases). Aeroplanes for instance, can fly on autopilot, but we still need the human pilot to be ready to take over in case the autopilot fails, or in case of emergency.
* *Secondly*, humans will need to supervise machines and to coordinate tasks (think of the factory where machines execute the tasks, humans no longer need to do repetitive work, but still need to supervise machines.
* *Thirdly*, humans will enhance their intelligence from the data they obtain from AI. There are many cases where humans' intelligence or skills were enhanced by AI, among which, the above discussed AI developments in chess beating Kasparov, and the AI developments, which resulted in the AlphaGo beating the Go game champion. In both cases, the AI learned to perform better than the human player, but the result of which was that human players could use AI to enhance their skill. They would observe the AI game, analyse its decisions and moves and learn from it.

So, what could all this mean for coaching? The AI coach can become better than the human coach at making rational, emotion-free judgement about actions and events (although it does involve the programmer's biases in the first place). It can be helpful for collecting client data based on the clients' responses, and identifying patterns of behaviour, which could help clients set an action plan for achieving their goals. The AI coach could eventually take over such tasks and perform them reliably and efficiently. Could AI then replace the human coach? There are at least two possible scenarios about the future of AI coaching.

The first scenario is that AI will eventually replace the human coach. Speaking to a machine might inspire openness and disinhibition, and in this sense, it can achieve a different kind of trust than speaking to a human coach. The human coach may not judge, but at the same time a human can't be completely impartial. The AI definitely doesn't judge, as it doesn't have feelings. The coachee can say anything, an embarrassing story, reveal secret thoughts, ideas, and emotions.

Aside from anonymity and trust, AI will only become better at analysing our responses and accurately calculating the best possible options for solving the coaching problem. Of course, what the human coach has, which the AI is devoid of, is emotional intelligence (EI). Can AI ever give us the feeling it

really understands our emotions, or that it can read between the lines and identify a bitterness in a comment that was intended to sound positive, or that it can
access our emotions and connect with own personal experiences, and create
a strong relationship? Can AI ever use intuition like a human does? With developments in face recognition, AI coaching bots could analyse coachees' facial
expression and body language to detect emotional states, at least to some extent
in the near future. By giving AI agents a humanoid presence, we could even
reach a point where the difference between the human and AI coach is much
reduced, supporting the acceptance of having a digital coach, rather than
a human one. AI-powered coaching, that is less focused on the coaching relationship and on transformation coaching, but it is more focused on shorter,
more transactional forms of coaching, is certainly possible. Even though it may
be hard to predict the different paths a coaching conversation might take and to
teach machines all those different paths, Machine Learning will for sure, enable
machines to learn an increasing range of contents and it will enable AI conversational interfaces to coach on more types of coaching issues. It may well be that
they will become good enough to perform simple, structured coaching models,
to analyse coachees' responses and offer appropriate and empathetic responses,
thereby replacing some human coaches. AI could at least replace the less skilled
human coach (Clutterbuck et al., 2019).

The implications of AI replacing human coaches would be significant. AI
coaching would entail that coaching is accessible to everyone, as the costs would
be greatly reduced as compared to coaching received by a human. Rather than
a few selected employees, coaching could become accessible to an entire company, with AI-coaching bots providing continuous support, or as and when it's
needed. The challenges that AI could create are also not negligible. Firstly, ethical questions would arise about data security. What happens to the data that is
exchanged with a chatbot? Are coaching chatbots encrypted? How can they
improve unless coaching conversations are used for machines to learn? Secondly,
the algorithms behind chatbots can be biased, as they develop based on the data
they are trained on. Think of the example of Microsoft's Tay chatbot, which
was taught to be racist. Examples such as this, emphasize the need for developers
to be very aware of any cognitive biases that could be transferred to their chatbots and to carefully consider how to train unbiased chatbots.

The second scenario is that AI can take over various tasks within the coaching
process, but it can't entirely replace the human coach. AI may perform both:

- Administrative tasks: scheduling appointments, matching and billing, but
  also
- Coaching tasks: giving pre-coaching questionnaires, identifying and suggesting relevant resources, analysing responses, identifying behavioural patterns
  and suggesting actions and holding simple coaching conversations on specific topics based on structured coaching models, to be followed up by the
  human coach.

Clearly, the human coach's role is much more holistic than collecting and analysing client data to suggest the actions with the highest probability of success to clients. Whilst such tasks can be extremely useful in supporting clients' decision-making, the human coach offers empathy, human connection, collaboration, and intuition, all of which, are necessary to account for human complexity. The coaching client is not just a rational being that will set a goal and take all the necessary actions to implement it. Emotions, interpersonal relationships, conflicting interests and needs, identity, personality and past experience can interfere with rational decision-making. Implementing actions can go wrong or it can be inconsistent. The client could revert to old behavioural patterns. The role of the human coach is to help the client to understand and to cope with emotions, and to improve her problem-solving skill that will enable her to solve future problems in a self-directed way. In carrying out administrative, and certain analytical tasks, AI augments the human coach. The human coach can benefit from AI automated processes and analytics to work more efficiently, and to use the data obtained from AI to quickly gain insights into the client's issue. The human coach then can focus on the human element: the coaching relationship, intuition, and empathy. The challenge in this scenario is for the coach to learn to collaborate with AI and to achieve a symbiotic relationship with it, where human and AI coach work together as partners (see Licklider, 1960). The AI enhances the human coach's capabilities, adding accuracy and efficiency, while allowing room for the coach to focus on empathy, rapport, and trust building. Such a symbiosis between coach and AI will imply that the accuracy and reliability of analysis based on AI meets the emotional intelligence and intuition of the coach. Objectivity meets subjectivity, both of which are important for coaching; staying impartial and objectively analysing a coaching problem, whilst also showing empathy, building trust, using own personal experiences. This powerful combination would make coaching even more valuable and attractive.

Question for reflection: Reflect 15 years into the future. What are the skills and capabilities of the human coach working with AI?

AI could be a significant help for team coaching. It could support the team coach, by analysing and gathering data of each team member, performing comparisons, noting changes in performance, and informing the human coach. AI could also play an important role in coach supervision and training. Imagine a coach training, where trainees are coaching one another to practice the role of the coach. AI could analyse their responses to their 'client' and help them reflect and improve their techniques. In supervision, supervisor and coach could review coaching sessions using the analytical data provided by AI.

Giving the exponential developments in AI, these scenarios are not utopic. Aspects of the options discussed are already available. Along with these new possibilities, there are potential risks, such as data breaches and biases that could cause harm to coaching clients. Thus, the task of the coach is to become aware of the options and the threats, and to take necessary steps to ensure the client's security. In learning to work with AI, coaches need to understand it and to find ways that will enhance their work. Leaving fear and suspicion behind is part of this task, if coaching is to forge ahead.

References

Axelsson, A. S., Abelin, A., Heldal, I., Schroeder, R., & Widerström, J. (2001). Cubes in the cube: A Comparison of a puzzle-solving task in a virtual and a real environment. *CyberPsychology & Behavior*, 4 (2), 279–286.

Bailey, S. K. T., Johnson, C. I., Schroeder, B. L., & Marraffino, M. D. (2017). Using virtual reality for training maintenance procedures. *Interservice/Industry Training, Simulation, and Education Conference (I/ITSEC) 2017*.

Barrett, M. & Blackledge, J. (2012). Evaluation of a prototype desktop virtual reality model developed to enhance electrical safety and design in the built environment. *ISAST Transactions on Computing and Intelligent Systems*, 3 (3), 1–10.

Bowman, D. A., Ragan, E. D., Sowndararajan, A., & Kopper, R. (2010). *The effects of higher levels of immersion on procedure memorization performance and implications for educational virtual environments*. Center for Human-Computer Interaction Department of Computer Science Virginia Tech Blacksburg, VA.

Clutterbuck, D. A., Gannon, J., Hayes, S., Iordanou, I., Lowe, K., & MacKie, D. (2019). *The practitioner's handbook of team coaching*. Oxford and New York: Routledge.

Dede, C., Salzman, M., Loftin, R. B., & Ash, K. (1997). Using virtual reality technology to convey abstract scientific concepts. In M. J. Jacobson & R. B. Kozma (Eds.) *Learning the sciences of the 21st century: research, design and implementing advanced technology learning environments* (pp. 361–413). Mahwah, NJ: Erlbaum.

Ebermann, D. (2017). Coaching im Digitalen Wandel. *Coaching Magazin*, Edition 1. Online resource: www.coaching-magazin.de/beruf-coach/coaching-digitaler-wandel-teil-1.

Ekstrand, C., Jamal, A., Ngyuen, R., Kudryk, A., Mann, J., & Mendez, I. (2018). Immersive and interactive virtual reality to improve learning and retention of neuroanatomy in medical students: A randomized controlled study. *CMAJ Open*, 6 (1), 103–109.

Freeman, J., Lessiter, J., Pugh, K., & Keogh, E. (2005). When presence and emotion are related, and when they are not. *Proceedings of the Conference at Presence 2005*, London.

Frey, C. B. & Osborne, M. A. (2013). The future of employment: How susceptible are jobs to computerisation? *Oxford Martin Programme on Technology and Employment*. Oxford Martin School, University of Oxford, UK.

Havranek, M., Langer, N., Cheetham, M., & Jäncke, L. (2012). Perspective and agency during video gaming influences spatial presence experience and brain activation patterns. *Behavioral and Brain Functions*, 8 (1), 34.

Hoffman, H. G., Richards, T., Coda, B., Richards, A., & Sharar, S. R. (2003). The illusion of presence in immersive virtual reality during an fMRI brain scan. *CyberPsychology & Behavior*, 6 (2), 127–131.

Licklider, J. C. R. (1960). Man-computer symbiosis. *IRE Transactions on Human Factors in Electronics*, March, Vol. HFE-1 (1), 4–11.

McCarthy, J. (1959). Programs with common sense. In: *Proceedings of the Teddington Conference on the Mechanization of Thought Processes*, 756–791. London: Her Majesty's Stationery Office.

Minsky, M. (1967). *Computation: Finite and infinite machines*. Englewood Cliffs, NJ: Prentice-Hall.

Minsky, M. (1970). Form and content in computer science. *Journal of the Association for Computer Machinery*, 17 (2), 197–215.

Newell, A. & Simon, H. (1956). The logic theory machine: A complex information-processing system. *IRE Transactions on Information Theory IT2*, 61–79.

Parmar, D. (2017). *Evaluating the effects of immersive embodied interaction on cognition in virtual reality*. Doctoral dissertation, Clemson University, South Carolina, US.

Piaget, J. (1964). Cognitive development in children: Piaget development and learning. *Journal of Research in Science Teaching*, 2 (3), 176–186.

Pulijala, Y., Pears, M., Ma, M, & Peebles, D. (2018). Effectiveness of immersive Virtual Reality in surgical training – A randomized controlled trial. Journal of Oral Maxillofacial Surgery, 76(5), 1065–1072.

Sankaranarayanan, G., Wooley, L., Hogg, D. et al. (2018). Immersive virtual reality-based training improves response in a simulated operating room fire scenario. *Surgical Endoscopy*, 32, 3439–3449.

Simon, A. H. (1957). *Models of man, social and rational: Mathematical essays on rational human behavior in a social setting*. New York: John Wiley & Sons.

Slater, M. & Wilbur, S. (1997). A Framework for Immersive Virtual Environments (FIVE): Speculations on the role of presence in virtual environments. *Presence Teleoperators & Virtual Environments*, 6 (6), 603–616. Accessed online at http://citeseerx.ist.psu.edu/view doc/download?doi=10.1.1.472.622&rep=rep1&type=pdf.

Stevens, J. A. & Kincaid, J. P. (2015). The relationship between presence and performance in virtual simulation training. *Open Journal of Modelling and Simulation*, 3, 41–48.

Varela, F., Thomson, E., & Rosch, E. (1991). *The embodied mind: Cognitive science and human experience*. Cambridge, MA: MIT Press.

Winn, W. D., Windschitl, M., Fruland, R., Hedley, N., & Postner, L. (2001, April). Learning science in an immersive virtual environment. *Paper presented at the annual meeting of the American Educational Research Association*, Seattle, WA.

Witmer, B. & Singer, M. (1998). Measuring presence in virtual environments: A presence questionnaire. *Presence*, 7, 225–240.

Woods, N. (2018). *Coaching and the use of technology*. Research paper, Sydney Business School, University of Wollongong, Australia.

Zhang, K., Chen, J., Suo, J., Chen, J., Liu, X., & Gao, L. (2017). Design and implementation of fire safety education system on campus based on virtual reality technology. *2017 Federated Conference on Computer Science and Information Systems (FedCSIS)*, Prague, Czech Republic.

Websites
VR applications

1. Anyworld https://anyworld.com
2. AltspaceVR https://altvr.com/
3. Bigscreen VR http://bigscreenvr.com/
4. Engage https://engagevr.io/
5. Facebook Spaces www.facebook.com/spaces

6. Google Earth VR https://vr.google.com/earth/
7. Google Earth Tour Creator https://vr.google.com/tourcreator/
8. Google Expeditions VR https://play.google.com/store/apps/details?id=com.google.vr.expeditions&hl=en
9. InstaVR www.instavr.co/
10. LearnBrite www2.learnbrite.com/
11. MeetingRoom.io https://meetingroom.io/
12. MeetinVR http://meetinvr.net/
13. Mindshow www.mindshow.com/
14. Ovation www.ovationvr.com/
15. Rec Room https://rec.net/
16. Roomful https://roomful.net/
17. Rumii www.rumii.net/landing
18. SonoVR http://sonovr.com/
19. TiltBrush www.tiltbrush.com/
20. Trint https://trint.com/
21. Virtway Events www.virtwayevents.com/
22. VR Chat https://vrchat.net/
23. VR Mood Booster www.captainvr.nl/product/reduceer-stress-op-de-werkvloer
24. Wander VR www.oculus.com/experiences/go/1887977017892765/?locale=en_US

AI applications

1. BRIN www.welcome.ai/tech/personal-assistant/brin-ai-business-advisor-app
2. Butterfly www.butterfly.ai/</URI>
3. Charlie www.welcome.ai/boldr
4. Coach Amanda https://leadx.org/hr-ai-chatbot-coach
5. CoachBot www.saberr.com/coachbot
6. IBM® Watson™ Career Coach www.ibm.com/talent-management/career-coach
7. IThrive http://sonovr.com/
8. LeaderAmp www.leaderamp.com/
9. Orai www.orai.com/
10. PocketConfidant https://pocketconfidant.com/
11. Tess www.x2ai.com/
12. Woebot https://woebot.io/
13. Wysa www.wysa.io/

5

THE DIGITAL COACH

Balancing media capabilities and coaching skills

The coaching experience is transformed by digital media

Media are central to the coaching process. Whether traditional face-to-face conversations or technology-mediated conversations at a distance, language – verbal or written – is what makes coaching possible in the first place. It's the basic medium of coaching. In addition to this, different media options facilitate coaching communication messages. These media are not only content transmitters, but they also play a role in the coaching interaction and influence its dynamics. Kozma (1991) argued that, depending on their capabilities, different media may enable (or they might constrain) a method – in our case, the coaching method. In the previous chapters we explored how different communication media, such as the telephone, video, and synchronous and asynchronous text-based communication facilitate the coaching conversation as well as how different coaching software may be used to enhance different phases of the coaching process. As we've seen in previous chapters, different digital media may support rapport building and intimacy, allow space for client reflection and enhance problem-solving processes. Various media attributes may play a role in the coaching communication, for instance:

- Asynchronous communication may enhance clients' reflection, it may allow crafted, well-thought out responses, and reduce judgement and power dynamics.
- Auditory-verbal communication can enhance the focus on the content of the conversation.
- Visual communication potentially supports rapport building and trust.
- Supporting text tools help to guide clients in their problem-solving processes.

- Supporting visual tools could provide the coach deeper insights into clients' issue and they can be useful in analysing and reflecting on the coaching problem, simulating solutions and practicing new behaviours.

A wide spectrum of digital tools is available in the market and each of them has its pros and cons. Not only rich media can be usefully employed in coaching, as Daft and Lengel would have argued, but also lean, text media can be used to facilitate the coaching communication and to support coaching processes. Moreover, coaches' preferences and choices of different media vary, change over time, and research evidence shows differences in this respect. For instance, Frazee's qualitative study (2008), found that coaches prefer using email to video conferencing, whilst the Sherpa Executive Coaching Survey reported an increase in coaches' preference of video conferencing in 2019 as compared to the previous years from 2012 onwards. A recent Delphi study with 15 coaches by Woods (2018) showed their preference for mobile- and web-based text communication, followed by audio and video communication, whilst also recognizing the potential that AI can have for supporting coaching processes.

However, users' media experiences are not only influenced by the objective capabilities of the media, but also by their *subjective perceptions* of media capabilities (Ihde, 1979). From a phenomenological point of view, our experience of the world changes when using different media. With his concept of Being-in-the-world, Heidegger (1962) noted that the human being makes sense of things, while essentially always being situated and immersed in the world. This relation between human and lifeworld can be mediated through technology. In its mediating role, technology alters or transforms human experience (Ihde, 1979). Even if both, rich and lean media can be viable in mediating interpersonal communication, different media create different coaching experiences. There is a difference between a video-based coaching conversation in a video call, a dialogue where communication is reduced to the written word, and a dialogue where clients are represented through avatars in a virtual, rather than a physical world. The role of technological media as the means to human experience has been explained by Don Ihde's (1979) different types of human-technology relations:

Embodiment relations: In this type of symbiotic human-technology relation, technology becomes perceptually transparent (Ihde, 2013, p. 8), in the sense that it tends to withdraw from our awareness. Ihde (1979, 2013) used the characteristic example of the telescope, which creates a transformed view of the world and one that differs from the view one would see through their eyes only. In this example, one becomes less aware of the telescope, or otherwise said, the telescope becomes transparent as one sees *through* it (Ihde, 2013, p. 10). Transferring this to a coaching context, media become transparent in the awareness of the coaching pair as they become embodied. In this sense, the coach speaks *through* the telephone to the client, or sees the client *through* the screen in a video call. Or the client experiences a virtual world by manipulating the physical interface, that is the computer. While the client focuses on the computer, what she actually 'sees' is the virtual world that the technology transfers her to. In other words, the technology that mediates the coach's or the client's experience (the coaching dialogue or the visualization of the coaching issue) retracts to 'the background' as the coach or client embodies the technology.

Arguably, the more embodied a technology is, the more seamless the experience has the potential to be, in a way that we hardly notice the technology. For instance, a Head Mounted Display might become more perceptually transparent and can thus, allow a more immersive experience in a virtual environment, than when looking at the virtual world on a flat computer screen. The Head Mounted Display amplifies the experience of a virtual environment.

There is also an obvious embodiment relation between the coaching client and the avatar, particularly in immersive Virtual Reality technology where the client embodies an avatar (first-person perspective) to explore and interact with a virtual world. The human client's physical head and hands movements are represented without time lag in the virtual environment, creating an illusion of 'being' there.

The perceptual transparency of media however, might be affected by their performance and ease of use. The higher the technical quality and user-friendliness of the medium, the more transparent the experience of the medium is likely to become, whilst technical limitations or complex use can make us perceptually aware of the medium. A technical disruption due to a low internet connection during a video call, poor image quality, a Head Mounted Display feeling heavy and uncomfortable or causing nausea, or the learning curve involved in mastering the right finger taps in the HoloLens are all examples where the 'symbiosis' of human and technology is likely to be disturbed.

> *Question for reflection*: Does the embodiment relation only depend on the medium's performance and technical quality?

Hermeneutic relations: A hermeneutic relation according to Ihde (1979) involves reading and interpreting the technology, which represents information about the world before we can apply the information, as for instance, a thermometer or a compass. Coaching tools that involve hermeneutic relations, include visualizations such as graphs, drawings, and progress charts, as well as text-based contents that represent information. For instance, in using a journaling software, the coaching client's journal entry requires interpretation by the coach to obtain insights into the client's emotional states and thought processes. The coach's relation to the medium is a hermeneutic one, as it involves reading the information that represents the client's world.

Text media reduce the coaching experience to written word. The client/coach is disembodied when using text-based media, as neither the body and face of the communication partner are visible, nor the voice can be used to convey meaning. On the other hand, the disembodiment that the client/coach experiences allows distance and thereby, space to reflect and articulate thoughts.

The hermeneutic human-technology relation in the context of coaching emphasizes the importance of clarity, methodical use, and structure of coaching media. What becomes important for instance, when text-based question sets are used to support clients' reflection processes is, how understandable, precise, and clear the questions are, and how they are structured based on coaching methodology to support clients' outcome-oriented reflection processes.

Alterity relations: Ihde (1990) discussed alterity relations that emerge in technologies that display a 'quasi-other' quality and behaviour. In the example of avatar-based coaching, to be able to act within a virtual world, the coaching client needs to merge with the avatar. In a sense, this is a clear embodiment relation between the coaching client and the avatar, particularly in immersive Virtual Reality technology where the client embodies an avatar from a first-person perspective. On the other hand, the relation between human and avatar can also be seen as an alterity relation. In the ProReal software, an avatar-based virtual environment designed for coaching and counselling, coaching clients view the representation of themselves (their avatar) from a first- or a third-person perspective, and they may give their avatar a colour, a size, a posture, and a caption. These attributes are supposed to match clients' emotional state. The avatar becomes a technological extension of the client, a 'quasi-other' which resembles the client, but it might display a different behaviour than the client would display in the physical world.

> *Question for reflection*: This relation can also be reversed: How might clients' cognitive or emotional states change if clients change the appearance of their avatar to match their desired state? For instance, could creating a very tall avatar give the client a feeling of confidence? In both cases, the experience of 'being' in the virtual world is shaped by the connection between the client and the avatar.

A chatbot is another clear example of what Ihde sees as 'quasi-other'. Clients' interactions with coaching chatbots (e.g. PocketConfidant, Butterfly.ai, CoachOtto, Saberr) can be understood as alterity interactions, because chatbots are experienced as something more than just a computer program. Specifically, they may be experienced as having a humanoid presence, an autonomy (e.g. the autonomy to ask reflective questions) and perhaps in the future, as having a consciousness. The implication of chatbots and avatars in coaching is that, quasi-otherness influences the client's relation to technology, which then shapes the coaching experience. For instance, the anonymity, humanoid presence and reaction of the chatbot to the client could possibly encourage the client's openness and self-disclosure, or the representation of the client as an avatar and seeing one's avatar interact with the virtual world could potentially provide new insights about oneself.

To summarize, digital media can have transformative consequences to the coaching experience. Media affect our perceptions and experiences with them in various ways. The sensory qualities of different media may amplify, or they may reduce the coaching experience, and our perceptual awareness of digital media differs based on the extent to which technology is embodied. The coaching experience also depends on whether the medium is used as a means to interpret information (text-based tools, images, Augmented Reality) or as an interaction with the technological 'other' (chatbots, virtual assistants). These different human-technology relations of course, may coexist (e.g. avatars as embodiment and as technological 'other') and together shape our mediated coaching experience.[1]

Question for reflection: How powerful is the coach and client in their relations with technology?

Is it the media or coaching skill?

As discussed previously, in their interaction with technology, coach and client may embody media and become almost unaware of them, they may use media to access and apply information, or to interact with a quasi-other that mirrors their emotional state. The interaction with different media might bring to surface different personas, as for instance, coach and client might behave differently in an online text-based interaction than a video-based communication.

Whilst the interaction with media transforms subjective perception and experience of them, objective media capabilities and performance can't be changed. For instance, video communication implies that few contextual cues are accommodated and that whilst non-verbal cues are supported, the more subtle non-verbal messages don't come through. Whilst the continuous advancements in technology are improving the performance of video technology, many aspects won't be in the control of the coaching pair. In the example of video-based communication, the power of the internet connection and the picture quality during the coaching session are out of the coach's hands. On the other hand however, in the same example, it's also about *how* the webcam is placed, allowing a view of the coach's head and upper body and to a certain extent, the background. In this sense, it's not only about *which* media are used and *what* their capabilities are, but to an extent, it's also about *how* they are used. Their successful use in coaching requires the coach's technological competencies. As one coach described:

> Being a master of the medium can help us craft a dynamic coaching space that strives for the best possible interaction.

> *(Source: Kanatouri, 2018)*

The interaction with technology within a coaching context requires that the coach has an affinity to technology and is accustomed to using digital media. One side of the coin is that the media capabilities will influence the coaching communication, its flow, dynamics, rapport and trust building, personas that come through and what is shared. The performance of the medium and its ease of use are certainly crucial for seamless communication. Technical disruptions, low picture quality, or a software that is complex to navigate can disturb this flow and seamlessness. The other side of the coin is however, that the relation between coach/client and technology is not only shaped by the fixed capabilities of digital media, but it's also influenced by the skill and experience with them. Carlson and Zmud (1999)'s study and subsequent empirical studies (a.o. D'Urso & Rains, 2008; Timmermann & Madhava-peddi, 2007) demonstrated that users' experience with a medium can affect their perception of the medium's richness. In turn, subjective evaluations towards a medium could affect the coaching experience. An example here is that, even though communication media that rely on limited sensory channels could slow down rapport building, they don't prevent it (Walther, 1992). Walther (1992) proposed that communicators adapt to the sensory cues that are available to them in order to establish rapport. Walther's proposition implies that users' perceptions of different media to support coaching depend on their level of technical skill, familiarity, and experiences made with the medium. Over time and experience with a medium, we become more comfortable, quick at using it, and ultimately less perceptually aware of the medium, as Ihde (1979) suggested. Our mediated communication with a person(s) becomes seamless, as if the medium wasn't in between us and our interlocutor. In this sense, media capabilities and performance are coupled with experience of and comfort with using these media. The technologically competent coach possesses the following:

- First, the coach is familiar with the medium in use: What are the medium's strengths, its weaknesses, its implications for the coaching conversation?
- Second, the coach is able to navigate and use a tool comfortably, without the tool becoming an obstacle to the coaching session. The coach needs to be able to troubleshoot within a session, in case of technical problems and disruptions, which can be frustrating for the client and for the coach, and to provide guidance to the client if needed.
- Third, the coach is aware of the ethical issues that may arise, takes appropriate measures to preserve the client's data privacy and confidentiality (e.g. by using encrypted software), and to advise the client accordingly.
- Fourth, having an overview of the different media available and understanding their capabilities can be helpful for the coach to select a suitable medium for their client's issue. The coach could be familiar with a range of different media, to have the option to alternate between them depending on the client's coaching issue, sensory and learning preferences, and

personality, or to combine media, and to bring into the coaching process different elements (e.g. visual, text-based, creative, cognitive). In a coach's own words:

> I think that coaches should be able to dance in the moment with their clients. For me, this means that that we need to reach a level of comfort with a range of communication media, because not only can we step into a medium that the client finds more comfortable, we can also harness the benefits of different media.
>
> *(Source: Kanatouri, 2018)*

The coaching competencies of the digital coach

Not only may the use of media affect the coaching experience, but as we've seen, the technological competencies of the coach can influence the smoothness of the coaching conversation and they can allow the coach to exploit the digital palette. Beyond technological competencies, adapting coaching skill to the digital form of coaching is potentially critical.

Adapting to sensory cues: enhanced listening competencies

In working with new media, the challenge that the coach faces is that, of managing his or her own presence, and also understanding the client's challenges and intentions, evaluating the client's emotional states, demonstrating empathy and guiding the problem-solving process, with reduced sensory data. If the coaching conversation is telephone-based, the coach manages his presence through the sound of his voice and choice of words. His perception of the client and the coaching problem is based on listening:

> I'm trained to be aware and to recognize in detail the acoustics data I get. So, I get a very full picture of emotional reactions of a person.
>
> *(Source: Kanatouri, 2018)*

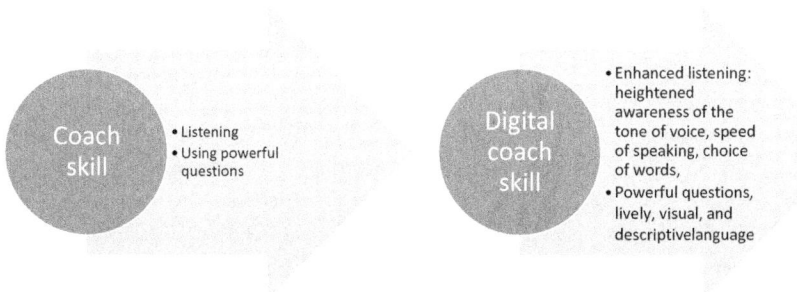

Coach skill
- Listening
- Using powerful questions

Digital coach skill
- Enhanced listening: heightened awareness of the tone of voice, speed of speaking, choice of words,
- Powerful questions, lively, visual, and descriptivelanguage

FIGURE 5.1   The enhanced skills of the digital coach

Certainly, the use of language and listening are the skills required by every coach, coaching face-to-face or in the virtual space. These coaching tasks however, need a certain adaptation when working remotely. When auditory-verbal cues are the only cues available in the coaching conversation, they have to compensate for the missing ones – for the visual cues, for the contextual information and the missing physical presence and proximity to the client. All coaches have to listen attentively, this is a core coaching competency. When the information they have from the client can only be obtained by listening however, the digital coach has to develop a heightened attentiveness. The coach's listening skill needs to be adapted and enhanced, due to the higher challenge.

Body language conveys important information about one's thoughts and emotions. When visual cues are missing as in telephone- or text-based communication, the coach faces the additional challenge to understand the client's emotional state.

BOX 5.1 THE MATCH/MISMATCH OF BODY LANGUAGE AND WORDS

John has been coaching his clients in a face-to-face mode for several years. Two weeks ago, John asked one of his clients as she entered the room:
'How are you doing Jane?'

'I am fine,' Jane responded, although in a very breezy way. In her unguarded moments, John could see however, that something was deeply troubling her. By observing Jane, John was aware of the mismatch of her body language and her words.

Recently, he has been coaching some of his clients via telephone, which has allowed him and his clients to choose a convenient time for coaching, to reduce travel time and cost. While John appreciates the practicality of coaching via the phone, he feels that not having visual contact to the client creates a challenge for understanding the client's emotional state. In one of his telephone coaching sessions, John was surprised that his client suddenly became very silent and started crying, when he thought that the client was feeling well.

Source: Kanatouri (2018)

As demonstrated in Box 5.1, the client's explicit messages are conflicting with her implicit messages, conveyed through non-verbal cues. When all cues, visual, auditory-verbal, contextual cues are available, the coach has the opportunity to cross-check the explicit and the implicit communication messages that are intentionally or sometimes unintentionally expressed. When coaching via the phone however, the coach has to do more than active listening. The coach needs to listen not only to the words used, but also the tone of the client's voice, the speed of speech, the pitch of the client's voice, the breathing patterns, even to the silences. So, the coach might gain information about the client's emotional state from how the client says 'I am fine' as in the above example. Speaking very quickly might suggest a possible nervousness, or depending on the context, a silence on the other end of the phone could betray an emotionally charged situation for the client.

The risk, of course, is misinterpreting these clues. As in the above example, the client started crying, to the coach's surprise. The coach had misinterpreted the client's implicit communication messages, and hadn't identified the mismatch between the communicated explicit and implicit messages. The coach's listening skill is very important, particularly in the virtual space and adapting this skill to working remotely is necessary to gain as much as possible a complete picture of the client.

A comparable adaptation is needed for facilitating coaching conversations in written form. Instead of listening, the coach must read and examine very carefully, the client's descriptions and reasoning, and to read what is between the lines. The risk of misinterpretation in this form of communication is high, as the client's presence is limited to the words they share. Thus, attentiveness to language and to the subtle cues in the client's expression is crucial for compensating for the absence of face-to-face presence.

Adapting to sensory cues: using vivid, visual language

Using language skilfully is another important coaching skill. This involves asking powerful questions, with which to guide client's cognitive process. Similarly, the coach's skilful use of language is fundamental to the digital coaching process (Charbonneau, 2002; Clutterbuck & Hussain, 2010; Frazee, 2008). To compensate for the absence of sensory cues, for not seeing the client and experiencing her physical presence, digital coaching requires an even higher attentiveness to the coach's use of language. In a telephone-based conversation, the coach may ask the client who has suddenly gone quiet at the other end of the phone: 'If I could see your facial expression right now, what would I be seeing?' Just like attending to the client's words, voice, breathing patterns, and silences, digital coaches control their own voice and breathing patterns. They can use silence to support clients' reflection. They may use vivid, descriptive, and pictorial language, with visual metaphors and analogies to complement the point they are making, to provide an accurate description, and thereby to minimize the risk that clients misinterpret the message they are trying to convey. As one coach described:

> I say, you are playing an instrument. Your voice is an instrument. A wonderful instrument. And it is an instrument of a wizard in a certain sense. You can create such wonderful results. You can bring the client in

a very special mood. Trigger fantasies or create worlds, new points of viewing and so on. You can do it by your voice and you are an artist. Nothing else than an artist. The people must learn it. At first it's a little strange for them to pay so much attention to their ears and voice, but then it works.

(Source: Kanatouri, 2018)

When coaching via text, the use of descriptive and pictorial language becomes even more important, as any mistakes and misinterpretation can't easily be rectified. Coupled with the coaches' skilled use of language and imagery to colour the meaning of the words they use, is their knowledge of, and familiarity with tools that can complement their and their clients' verbal expression. Visual aids, such as simple emoticons may assist in clarifying the coach's and client's intentions and feeling or mood. There is growing empirical evidence, suggesting that the use of emoticons[2] in online text-based exchanges could support non-verbal communication (Utz, 2000; Walther & D'Addario, 2001). Avatars could be an alternative way to complement text-based communication and to graphically represent one's emotions (DiFiore et al., 2008; Neviarouskaya, Prendinger, & Ishizuka, 2010; Sánchez et al., 2014), and virtual two- or three-dimensional images of objects and shapes in virtual worlds can also support the use of metaphors and symbolizations to the process.

Question for reflection: Reflect on all the ways in which the coach working with technology might differ from the traditional, face-to-face coach.

Developing the digital coach: the value of training and supervision

We've discussed how the viability of digital coaching doesn't depend solely on the fixed characteristics of a communication medium, but also on coaches' level of technical skill and adaptation of coaching skills to working with technology. To adapt coaching competencies to digital coaching practices or to develop enhanced coaching competencies and technical skills, specialized training can be important for coaches working with technology. Specialized training thus, can cover several objectives:

• **It can provide an overview of the range of media and their potential**: Through specialized training, coaches may obtain an overview of the different types of digital media available for use across various coaching phases and tasks. Coaches should understand the range, but also the potential and the limitations or risks of different media. This knowledge can help them to select the medium that best suits their clients' preferences, type of issue, and needs. It would also increase understanding as to how different media can be combined during the coaching process, or how they can complement one another, as well as how to enhance the process.

- **It can suggest best practices for handling digital technologies**: Specialized training could increase coaches' confidence in using digital media, helping them learn to navigate easily and to communicate seamlessly with their client. Moreover, it can help to raise coaches' awareness of potential ethical issues that could arise when using technology and to increase their knowledge of how to protect their clients' data security.

- **It can support the development of practitioners' enhanced coaching competencies**: Training can be used to support coaches in adapting their coaching competencies to working with new media. Coaches could learn how to control their voice, to use vivid language, imagery, and metaphors, managing the coaching relationship in a virtual environment, and their virtual representation. As coaching is a professional helping approach, the use of digital media to facilitate the coaching process requires an underlying method. Coaching is not a casual, unstructured conversation. The coaching conversation is structured by a method that determines the coaching questions and the way these are asked. Thus, mediated communication should be guided by coaching methods and techniques, and the way these can be used may vary from medium to medium.

- **It may support the management of digital coaching practices**: Starting from the contracting and initial digital coaching sessions, training could support coaches in learning to manage clients' expectations. For instance, how much time is contracted when coaching via email? Does it mean that the coach is available 24/7 or at specific times? How to handle session cancellations (as cancelling online could potentially be easier to do – just a click away – than via telephone)? How could coaches increase their online presence and attract more clients? Training can take the coach from learning how to build rapport and trust in a digital coaching process during the initial phases of coaching, through to guiding the client's problem-solving process. How is rapport built in the virtual space? How can the coach enhance clients' reflection? Which techniques are possible? For instance, teleporting to an inspiring virtual environment and testing behaviours in a safe space, using telephone shadowing to support the client's implementation process, and tools, such as text-based coaching assignments to increase contact frequency to the client.

Online supervision could provide ongoing value for the practicing digital coach. Supervisor and coach could explore together the challenges and experiences of the coach in the same virtual space, in which the coaching sessions take place. For example, they could meet in a virtual world, where the coach can reconstruct the coaching process, reflect on the client's reactions and gain understanding as to how to optimize the process within this environment under the guidance of the supervisor.

Coping with ethical issues

Digital coaching may imply higher ethical risks than face-to-face coaching, as some digital media aren't secure and they could compromise data privacy. Being in a room with the coach is completely different than communicating online. Whilst the anonymity of online communication can give some clients a feeling of safety, many clients may be concerned about how secure the data they provide is. Such concerns could be damaging to the reputation and the perception of digital coaching. It is thus, important for coaching practitioners to address such issues and to ensure clients' data security and confidentiality.

While coaching associations have set their own codes of ethics for coaching practice, the aspect of technology and its ethical implications have been somewhat neglected. Aside from the ethical framework that has been created by the joint effort of the Online Therapy Institute and the Institute for Life Coach Training (Labardee et al., 2011), the ethical use of technology in coaching is not well covered. Threats to clients' safety can be eliminated by using encrypted software, protecting computers from viruses, and storing clients' data safely. Further ethical issues may arise when coach and client don't see each other. For instance, during telephone coaching sessions, the coach might get distracted by an email that pops up on his screen, and multitask, instead of giving the client full attention. Or the coach might want to record the session for later review, in which case the client should be informed in advance and give their consent. Coaches working with technology need to be aware of potential ethical issues that could arise and take necessary steps to avoid them.

Digital coaching as a conceptually distinct form of coaching

To summarize, adapting to mediated coaching practice means not only becoming familiar with media and developing an understanding of their capabilities, their potential, and their limitations, but also developing enhanced coaching skills, listening skills, and language skills (Kanatouri, 2018, p. 168). Whilst these core skills are common to any form of coaching, the digital coach compensates for the limited sensory cues by developing a heightened awareness for clients' tone of voice, speed of speaking, silent moments, choice of words, or by developing strong reading, writing, or verbal language skills, and using clear and descriptive language.

Even though the performance of digital media and their design can play a role in making them more 'transparent' and a seamless means to the coaching experience, it is also up to the coach's skill to overcome some of the challenges added by technology, such as the limited sensory information and lack of physical proximity.

A coaching practice that is adapted to new media makes methodologically structured use of coaching contents (Geißler, in prep.). This is achieved by the coach's expertise and skill, whether the medium involves predefined coaching contents, thus, it incorporates coaching expertise and methods, or it is content-free, but requires the coach's method and skill in order to effectively guide the client's reflection and problem-solving process. In both cases, the coaching methodology and skill are used to shape the media in use and to structure the coaching process.

The differences in digital coaching experiences that result from the coaching pair's relation to the medium, from the challenges and complexity added by technology, and the need for adapting core coaching skills to overcome challenges, point us to rethink the meaning of digital coaching as a *conceptually distinct form of coaching practice* from traditional, face-to-face coaching; a form of practice where the mediated experience alters the coaching interaction in ways that may challenge coaches, and call for them to develop enhanced skills (Kanatouri, in press).

As users accumulate experiences with a medium, but also with the topic and with the interlocutor, they develop 'knowledge bases' that allow them to encode and decode rich messages and to communicate effectively (Carlson and Zmud, 1999). This suggests that *it is* possible to adapt to the media in use and to develop strong relationships, despite limited sensory cues (Walther, 1992). Thus, a positive digital coaching experience – at least in terms of the coaching pair's satisfaction – doesn't depend solely on the fixed characteristics of the communication medium, for instance, its richness, synchronicity, elements etc. It could also depend on coaches' level of experience with the medium, technological skill, and adaptation of coaching skills to working with technology.

There are several issues to be addressed, if digital coaching practice is to mitigate its current challenges. Given that technology is a moving target, coaches need to stay up-to-date and make informed selection decisions out of the plethora of digital tools available. As we've seen, there is a wide spectrum of coaching tools to enrich the coaching conversation at different phases of the process. It is thus, important that they develop their ability to evaluate these different tools, in terms of their suitability for their clients' individual needs and preferences. Technology transforms aspects of the coaching experience and requires coaches to adapt their coaching skills to working remotely, so that technology is seamlessly integrated in coaching practice.

It is also important for practitioners to watch upcoming trends and to consider their potential influence in coaching practice. Even if AI doesn't replace the human coach, it can certainly be used to support particular aspects of the coaching process, especially carrying out diagnostics and analysis, and it could thereby, enhance the work of the coach. Virtual and Augmented Realities can enrich the coaching conversation and offer options that are not possible in a face-to-face setting. They can in a way expand coaching practice, allowing the client to live lifelike situations, to teleport and immerse in imaginary worlds, or to take a fresh perspective of a constellation. The digital coach, or the coach who intends to work with technology needs to be aware of these new technologies, to understand their potential for coaching, and to learn to work with them. Over time, as the practitioner gains more experience in using technology, designing coaching software and teaching AI will become increasingly focused on capabilities and contents that will complement and augment the work of the coach and will lead to positive coaching outcomes. As new technologies become adopted, coaching clients' expectations are also likely to change and to reflect in their expected conditions of receiving coaching. To prepare, it will also be of advantage for coaches to be familiar and comfortable with these technologies.

Offering specialized training is a useful means for coaches to evaluate the different tools, but also to adapt their coaching and technical skills, to understand how to build rapport via distance and to optimize coaching practice through digital media. Ethical issues that could arise through the use of technology should not be neglected. They should be considered as part of the coach training curriculum.

Beyond ethical risks that need to be avoided and addressed, technology shouldn't be seen as a threat for coaching. Whilst the myriad of mobile coaching apps and web-based tools available don't all promise quality and serious coaching, there are tools that offer great potential for a real enrichment in coaching. Technology doesn't necessarily make coaching 'cheap', nor does it compromise its quality. Successful outcomes *can* be achieved through digital coaching.

Technology is also not panacea. Using the latest technology, won't make you a good coach. Being a skilled coach and developing additional skills to adapt to the tool that mediates the coaching conversation and process is the key. Embracing technology, rather than fearing it, is important for understanding how to exploit technology in a way that enriches the coaching interaction.

Notes

1 A slightly different version of the above discussion of Ihde's (1979) human-technology relations in a coaching context have been published in: Kanatouri, S. (2020) Digitales Coaching. In: C. Rauen (Ed.) *Handbuch Coaching*. (4. Edition in prep.) Göttingen, Hogrefe.
2 Emoticons are graphic representations of facial expressions that can be embedded in email and synchronous text-chat messages.

References

Anthony, K. & Nagel, D. A. (2009). *Ethical framework for the use of technology in coaching*. The Online Therapy Institute/Institute for Life Coach Training (2009). Retrieved from: http://onlinetherapyinstitute.com/ethical-framework-for-the-use-of-technology-in-coaching/.

Carlson, J. R. & Zmud, R. W. (1999). Channel expansion theory and the experiential nature of media richness perceptions. *The Academy of Management Journal*, 42(2), 153–170.

Charbonneau, M. A. (2002). *Participant self-perception about the cause of behavior change from a program of executive coaching.* Unpublished doctoral dissertation, Alliant International University, Los Angeles, CA.

Clutterbuck, D. & Hussain, Z. (Eds.) (2010). *Virtual coach, virtual mentor.* Charlotte, NC: Information Age Publishing.

D'Urso, S. C. & Rains, S. A. (2008). Examining the scope of channel expansion: A test of channel expansion theory with new and traditional communication media. *Management Communication Quarterly*, 21(4), 486–507.

DiFiore, F., Quax, P., Vanaken, C., Lamotte, W., & Van Reeth, F. (2008). Conveying emotions through facially animated avatars in networked virtual environments. In A. Egges, A. Kamphuis, & M. Overmars (Eds.) *Motion in games* (pp. 223–233). *MIG, lecture notes in computer science*, Vol. 5277. Berlin and Heidelberg: Springer.

Frazee, R. V. (2008). *E-coaching in organizations: A study of features, practices, and determinants of use.* Unpublished doctoral dissertation, San Diego University, USA.

Geißler, H. (in prep.). *Coaching: Methodische Gestaltung elektronischer Coachingmedien.* Hamburg: Studienbrief, Hamburger Fern-Hochschule (HFH).

Heidegger, M. (1962). *Being and time.* Oxford: Blackwell Publishing.

Ihde, D. (1979). *Technics and praxis* (1st edition). Dordrecht, Holland: D. Reidel Publishing.

Ihde, D. (1990). *Technology and the lifeworld: From garden to earth.* Bloomington, IN and Indianapolis, IN: Indiana University Press.

Ihde, D. (2013). *Technics and praxis* (2nd edition). Dordrecht, Boston, MA and London: D. Reidel Publishing.

Kanatouri, S. (2018). *Mapping the technology-assisted coaching field through the lens of an online community: An exploratory study.* Unpublished dissertation, Helmut-Schmidt University, Hamburg.

Kanatouri, S. (2020). Digitales coaching. In C. Rauen (Ed.) *Handbuch coaching* (4. Edition in prep.). Göttingen: Hogrefe.

Kozma, R. B. (1991). Learning with media. *Review of Educational Research*, 61(2), 179–211.

Labardee, L., Nagel, D. M., & Anthony, K. (2011). An ethical framework for the use of technology in coaching. Therapeutic Innovations in Light of Technology, 1 (4), 20–28.

Neviarouskaya, A., Prendinger, H., & Ishizuka, M. (2010). EmoHeart: Conveying emotions in second life based on affect sensing from text. *Advances in Human-Computer Interaction*, 2010(1), 1–13.

Sánchez, A., Starostenko, O., Medina, P., Cervantes, O., & Wan, W. (2014). Affordable development of animated avatars for conveying emotion in intelligent environments. In Z. C. Augusto & T. Zhang (Eds.), *Workshop Proceedings of the 10th International Conference on Intelligent Environments.* Amsterdam, Netherlands: IOS Press.

Sherpa Executive Coaching Survey. (2012). *Seventh annual report.* Retrieved from: www.associationforcoaching.com/media/uploads/publications/Survey-Executive-Coaching-2012.pdf.

Sherpa Executive Coaching Survey. (2019). *Fourtheenth annual report.* Retrieved from: www.sherpacoaching.com/pdf_files/2019_Executive_Coaching_Survey_Summary_Report.pdf.

Timmermann, S. E. & Madhavapeddi, S. N. (2007). Perceptions of organizational media richness: Channel expansion effects for electronic and traditional media across richness dimensions. *IEEE Transactions on Professional Communication*, 51(1), 18–32.

Utz, S. (2000). Social information processing in MUDs: The development of friendships in virtual worlds. *Journal of Online Behavior*, 1(1). Accessed on 30.12.19 www.sonja-utz.de/SIPMUDs_Utz.pdf.

Walther, J. B. (1992). Interpersonal effects in computer-mediated interaction: A relational perspective. *Communication Research*, 19(1), 52–90.

Walther, J. B. & D'Addario, K. P. (2001). The impacts of emoticons on message interpretation in computer-mediated communication. *Social Science Computer Review*, 19(3), 324–347.

Woods, N. (2018). *Coaching and the use of technology*. Master's thesis, University of Wollongong, Melbourne.

INDEX

Note: Page numbers in italics refer to figures; those in bold refer to tables.

Printed in Great Britain
by Amazon

75588828R00113